ALTAMAHA SUNSET

A Civil War Era Novel

By

GLENN OGDEN

To Wendy & Dick:
With Best Wishes,

3-5-2015

Dedication

To Lynne, my wife, soul mate and editor of my first book.

Note to Readers

This book is a work of historical fiction. All references to locations, individuals, groups or events in this story should be considered fictional—a product of the author's imagination. With that in mind, the author has attempted to show the fictional characters of the story in situations and environments that could have existed at that time of the story. The battles and references to historic persons included in the story are as factual as possible. Also, the dialog of the story has been simplified from the language of the era for easier reading.

Contents

Chapter 1

As we marched ever forward, the distant cannon fire reminded me of violent summer thunderstorms with bright flashing and booming thunder. But soon, the horrible sound of bullets whizzing by my ears and cannon balls crashing nearby quickly brought me back to a hellish reality.

Our regiment was two miles south of Franklin, Tennessee when we began to engage the enemy. It was mid-afternoon on a late November day. The ground, still damp and muddy from previous rains made the march even more difficult. Yankees were directly to our front in two strong defensive positions, one behind the other. Our attack would be over a large exposed open area. The enemy would see our every move and have clear and direct fire upon us.

As our lines continued to advance slowly uphill, enemy musket and cannon fire increased with our every step. Soldiers around me were beginning to fall but we kept moving forward. I cringed with fear at every explosion that pounded the ground around me. The flashes from their muskets and noise from their cannon overwhelmed my senses. Smoke swallowed the battlefield. It seemed like I was walking in a heavy fog but still seeing thousands of tiny flashes piercing through it. My eyes were tearing heavily. I couldn't think, all I could do was react.

"Come on men, keep moving. Keep moving forward. Let's kill those blue bastards. For God's sake men, keep moving," Lieutenant Hill shouted as he lead our attack.

I remember talking to myself as the bullets buzzed overhead, "We're out in the open. We can't see the enemy but he sees us. We're totally exposed. I'm going to die today. Lord help me, but I think I'm about to die."

In an instant, Lieutenant Hill was hit and down. I wanted to help him but I couldn't. I had to keep pushing forward. I refused to acknowledge what I had just seen. I didn't know how badly he was hurt or even if he was still alive. I just kept looking to the front. I had to keep moving. My buddies were falling. Our numbers were dwindling but we kept pushing forward.

The regiment marched into a violent inferno of death and hell. Our lines were becoming confused. I stopped briefly, aimed and fired my musket and then reloaded again. Fathers, uncles, brothers and sons were dropping everywhere around me. Those of us still alive continued our movement in that same deadly direction.

My brother Daniel was to my right. I could barely see him now. Only blurred movements were visible on either side of me. My eyes were burning from the smoke and powdered debris flying about.

"Daniel where are you? I can't see you."

"I'm right here Micah. I'm still with you. Keep moving buddy," he shouted.

It seemed like a dream to me--a very horrible dream which I knew would have a terrible ending. We continued up the long, slow hill. Just taking steps now was getting harder. My legs were aching and burning from the uphill surge.

The acrid smelling smoke was filling my lungs. My breathing had become difficult, labored. I was gasping, straining for clean air with every breath.

We finally reached the enemy positions and I could see those in blue who remained. Many had already retreated. Several soldiers were crouched over in the trench, paralyzed by fear. Others continued to fight as we moved into their lines.

Just to my front, an enemy soldier about thirty yards away was coming right at me. His bayonet was pointed forward. His face had no emotion. His eyes were dark and cold. I remember turning toward him, aiming my musket and pulling the trigger. The bullet pierced his chest, burrowing deeply inside. He dropped. His knees struck the ground first and then the rest of his body collapsed. His head snapped forward and his face crashed into the dirt. Blood was draining from the side of his body. It all happened in an instant. I winced, then continued on.

As I reached the top of another trench, three Yankees were bent down hiding next to the edge. I stopped suddenly and looked directly at them. I raised my musket and pointed it. When they realized they had my attention, they dropped their weapons and raised their arms in surrender. There was fear and uncertainty in their eyes. I jumped down and ran over to them.

"Stay down," I commanded. "Keep your head down and your arms up. Stay here until I come back." I grabbed their weapons and threw them outside the trench. I then quickly crawled out and continued moving forward with the rest of the regiment.

Hand-to-hand combat was all around me. It was happening so rapidly. There wasn't time to think, only to fight. I looked over quickly to Daniel who was still to my right. He jumped into a trench. An enemy soldier made a charge at him. He struck the soldier with his bayonet. An instant later, he clubbed another with the butt of his musket.

I heard Daniel scream and go down. "I'm hit," he shouted. Blood was spurting from his leg. I had a sick feeling in my stomach as I looked at him.

I rushed to where he was lying and then I felt a sharp pop on my left side. I too was knocked to the ground, hit by a bullet from an unknown assailant. I felt a burning sensation and then the pain. It was difficult to move. The pain was demanding that I stop but I had to get to Daniel even if I had to crawl.

"Are you okay? Can you get up?" I hollered at him.

He didn't look at me. "No Micah. I'm hit. I can't go any further. I think my leg is broken." I watched in amazement as he continued to load his musket and fire, even though he was lying on his side, in an awkward curled-up position. He wouldn't quit. He continued fighting.

"Micah, look out!" Daniel yelled a moment later. Out of the corner of my eye, to the left, he came. A soldier in blue charging directly at me with his musket lowered, bayonet attached and prepared to strike. He drew it back and then thrust it powerfully forward.

In an instant, the sun reflected off the metal of his bayonet and into my eyes. I felt the powerful movement of his knife cut deep into my chest. It pierced my heart.

I looked down at my chest. The tip of his musket with the bayonet attached was buried deeply inside. He then forcefully ripped it out as if I were a rag doll on a target post. All movement around me seemed to stop. Blood was flowing from a hole in my chest.

"I'm going to die now," I said to myself. "Please someone help me," I cried out. I screamed for anyone who could hear as I crumbled to the ground. The soldier who had attacked me was gone now, just a fleeting but horrible memory.

"Please help me," I yelled. A few moments later, help arrived. It was a familiar voice, one that I had heard many times before.

"Micah, Mister Micah, please wake up. You're having a nightmare. Wake up." I felt someone shaking me. I looked up and saw Malachi, the house attendant standing over me. Several others had joined him now. I looked at each of them and then slowly looked around the room. It wasn't a battlefield. It was my room. I was soaked in sweat and breathing heavily. Everything was spinning slowly. I began to sob.

"Micah, I'm going to ask Doctor Reynolds to stop by and see you tomorrow. Your nightmares seem to be getting worse. Maybe he can help you."

As I lay there, I stared up at Malachi, motionless but still with labored breathing. "Thank you dear friend," I said, in an exhausted, appreciative voice.

It was only a nightmare but it was a horrible and re-occurring one. It had seemed so real to me. Again, I was there, in the fight, in a struggle for survival. The violence was so close, swift and horrible. I continued to stare up at Malachi as my eyes began to slowly close. As I drifted back to sleep, I realized how thankful I was that it had not been real. It was only a dream. I was still alive. Today would not be my last.

Chapter 2

It was early fall, 1916 and I was living in the Peach Tree Home for the Elderly, in Savannah, Georgia. It was a pleasant, older home and had separate wings for white and Negro residents. Surrounding the home were large oak trees and lovely gardens with plants flowering in many colors. It was a nice, peaceful location away from the activity of the city. Outside, birds were chirping harmoniously and squirrels were busy collecting acorns for the coming winter season.

I was sitting quietly that morning, looking out my window watching nature pass by, something I did quite regularly. I enjoyed looking at deer, squirrels, rabbits, possums, birds of all varieties and many other critters that ventured within sight of the window. It was one of the few things that still gave me pleasure and comfort.

My mood was grim and I rarely shared thoughts or feelings with anyone. Outwardly, I was friendly or at least tried to be but mostly I kept to myself. I had been this way for some time now. I had lost nearly everyone who was close to me including several acquaintances in the home who had recently passed. My daughter, Ella, who I loved dearly, lived with her husband far away at a military post, Fort Riley, Kansas and I saw her only rarely. It seemed like my only friends now were memories and many of those were not that pleasant. I had become very much alone.

Dr. John Reynolds, the home physician, was making his rounds that morning and at the request of Malachi, had come to visit me. He was a tall, thin, middle-aged man, who slumped over a little when he walked. He had a beard with a grayish tint and seeing him reminded me of Abraham Lincoln. His speech was slow and his word selection deliberate. I might have thought him an old southern college professor, if I had met him in different circumstances.

"How are you feeling today Mr. Boden?" he asked.

"Oh, please call me Micah. Everyone calls me Micah and I prefer that. I'm about as well as can be expected, Doc. As you know, I still have that pain in my hip from the war. I get around okay I guess, though I still have some stiffness when I walk and need to use that bamboo cane you gave to me."

"I understand from Malachi that you've been having nightmares again. He says they're getting worse. Maybe I can help you."

"I've had them for years but they seem to be increasing, Doc. I would surely appreciate any help you can give."

"How old are you Micah?"

"I'm not sure. It's been a long time since I celebrated a birthday and I've stopped counting."

"You've been around for quite a while and I guess you've seen a lot haven't you?"

"Yes, I sure have. More than I want to remember."

"I've seen your medical records and noticed that you were in the war. My uncle, Charles Reynolds, also fought in the war and was wounded in a battle near Charleston. Since you and he were both from this area, I was wondering if you might have known him. I saw that you were both in the same unit, the 54th Georgia Infantry."

"Yes sir," I said, after considering his question for a moment. "I did know Charlie. He was a good soldier; a friend of mine. He was shot in the shoulder, I believe, in a battle at Grimball's Landing, near Charleston. I didn't see him after that or after the war and I don't know what happened to him. I heard some time back that maybe he didn't make it."

"After the battle he was moved to a hospital in Charleston, to care for his wounds," Dr. Reynolds then paused, "and he came down with pneumonia while he was there and passed away several weeks later."

"I'm really sorry to hear that. I considered Charlie a good friend. I didn't know him prior to joining the 54th but we became close while in the Savannah area. That was before we moved to Charleston Harbor in the summer of '63. I remember that Charlie had the sweetest singing voice in the regiment. We would gather around the campfire in the early evening just after eating and listen to him sing. His voice carried throughout the camp. He sang popular southern songs like, "Lorena," "Bonnie Blue Flag," and "When Johnny Comes Marching Home." I can still hear his voice now. Sometimes, we would all join in and sing along with him. It brought tears to your eyes just listening to him, getting caught up in the moment, thinking about our homes and families. War was very, very lonely at times. Do you sing Doc?"

"No Micah, I don't. I wish I did."

"Well Charlie could. Yes sir, he surely could sing. I remember it like yesterday. His pleasant voice on a warm summer's night was real soft on the ears."

"Micah, I appreciate your kind thoughts. I'd like to hear more about my uncle and your memories again, sometime soon. Maybe we can talk about what you're keeping bottled up inside that head of yours. It may help you to sleep better at night. What do you think? Do you want to try?"

"I'm willing Doc. I need to do something. I can't continue on like this. These dreams are so real and painful that sometimes, I think that maybe I'm going crazy. Sometimes I wish I would just die and get it over with."

Dr. Reynolds paused for a moment, looked at me carefully and then said, "I hope not. Not for a while. Not until you're ready, anyway." He paused again, "Micah, I'm writing a history about this area, its soldiers and units that participated in the war and I'd like to find out what you remember about that time. You may be able to add some detail to my research or at least, point me in the right direction. It may also help with your nightmares, being able to talk about what you saw."

"That would be fine, Doc. I'd enjoy talking with you when you have time."

"Well, why don't we make some time Micah? Can I come back and see you later this afternoon?"

"Sure. I'm here all day, anyway. I'm not going anywhere," I said with a smile and a chuckle. "I'm looking forward to your next visit Doc."

Chapter 3

Later that day, Dr. Reynolds came back to my room. "Good afternoon, Micah. I told you I'd be back. How're you feeling?" he asked, as he walked into my room and sat down in a well-worn but rather inviting leather wingback chair across from me. It was a gift from the family of a friend who had recently passed.

"I'm doing fine Doc. It's good to see you again."

"You were looking out the window when I came in. What was it that caught your eye?"

"Well, I'm just an old man passing time but I've been watching two squirrels quarreling over an acorn. Seems they're getting ready for winter early this year. There are plenty of other acorns out there and I've been watching for quite a while but I swear Doc, I don't know what's so special about that one acorn they're fighting over."

"Well, you know how that goes Micah. When someone has something, someone else usually wants it too. That's natural I suppose, even for squirrels. So Micah, I'd like to hear more about the war and anything else you can remember from that time. Do you feel like talking about it now?"

"I do Doc. It's been kind of quiet here today anyway. I have to tell you though, I've never shared this story with anyone. I believe it's time though. And, as you've said, maybe it'll help me with these nightmares I've been having lately. It probably won't hurt."

"I'm ready to listen and I'll take notes if you don't mind. I may even ask you a few questions."

"That's fine." I turned and looked out the window then began to speak, "Doc, this is my story. It's about my home, my family, an ill-advised love affair, that horrible war and what happened afterward. Are you still interested?"

"Indeed I am Micah. I want to hear about everything; everything you can remember."

"I swear, this story's true, every word of it. It's been many years since those events occurred but they're still very fresh in my mind. I think about them all the time now. Frankly, I don't have much else to do. They're with me during the day and I dream about them at night. The dreams are horrible sometimes. I wake up shaking and sweating. Sometimes I even wake up residents down the hall with my hollering and swearing, as you know. I can't really control that. When I go back in time, well, I'm there again, in the middle of it. I remember it so very vividly. I'm at the same places, with the same soldiers, in the same battles."

"Are the dreams that real Micah? Do they seem exactly as you remember them when you're awake?"

"They're very real, Doc. That's why they're so terrifying to me."

"I'm sorry for interrupting you Micah. Please continue."

I nodded to him. "The farm where I was born and raised, was in Southeastern Georgia, about 5-miles north of the Altamaha River and approximately fifty miles southwest of Savannah. Do you know that area Doc?"

"I sure do. I've visited some of my patients on their farms there."

"Well, it probably hasn't changed much in all this time.
The land was sparsely populated, mostly flat and almost completely covered with pine trees. It was quiet and peaceful before the war. The people were warm, friendly and caring, helping each other in their times of need."

My family included Jacob, my father; Sarah, my mother; Daniel, my older brother; Thomas, my younger brother; Pearl, our slave woman; Aliyah, Pearl's daughter and me. As you probably noticed, mother named her boys after folks in the Bible.

Our farm was small but we worked very hard to make it productive. Most of the land we cleared ourselves. We grew corn, green beans, tomatoes, peas, onions, watermelons and of course, cotton. We also had chickens, turkeys, pigs and some cows roaming around.

Our three room log house kept us comfortable. It was shaped like a large "U" with one living and eating area at the front and two rooms on each of the wings. It had a small fireplace in the living area. All the boys slept in one room; mother and father in the other. There was also a small cabin out behind the house for Pearl and Aliyah. We brought them in with us on especially cold nights.

Scattered on the farm were pecan trees which provided shade and the tasty pecans that mother included in her pies and other dishes. I still fondly remember sitting under my favorite pecan tree on a warm summer day, cracking the shells and then eating as many pecans as I could find, scattered about on the ground. Sometimes I would eat so many that I would go home with a stomach ache. Then I would have to listen to mother say, "I told you so."

The large stands of pine trees throughout the area provided the wood for building houses, barns, wagons and fences. In later years, the gum from the pine trees was used in making tar, pitch and turpentine. Tar and pitch were used in the building of ships. These items became very important to Georgia's economy.

Cotton was King of the South at this time. It was shipped to both the Northeastern United States and England for the manufacturing of textiles. Cotton was grown throughout Georgia. Rice was grown primarily on the coastal plains.

The farming of both of these was the main reason for the rapid expansion of slavery during the 18th and 19th centuries.

There weren't many slaves in our area though. They were mostly located near the coast for the farming of rice, which required large numbers of slaves and very long work days. Unfortunately, many slaves died due to the harsh conditions, illness and disease. Slavery was also common in the upper middle part of the state where the large cotton plantations were located. Even though slaves were bought and sold in markets in Savannah, we didn't realize the cruelty that was occurring elsewhere. Looking back now, maybe we should have known more. Father shielded us from much of it as we were growing up. Hopefully, God will forgive us for this legacy.

The success of our farming from year to year was unpredictable. We couldn't always count on sufficient rain, moderate weather or fruitful crops each and every growing season, so we planned carefully and we conserved. That was key to our survival.

Care of our animals was also very important. We worked hard to keep them healthy and free of disease. They had to be protected from predators, severe weather and fire. They provided us with eggs, milk, poultry, pork and beef.

Before I was born, a nearby farmer named John severely injured his leg in an accident while clearing trees from his land. Because of this, he could no longer work his farm like he had done previously. He and his wife were childless and had no family in the immediate area. He had two slaves on the farm named Pearl and Jeremiah.

Father and John knew each other well being neighbors and members of the church. They were good friends. Father offered to help John with the farm after his injury. That's what neighbors did back then. My father worked not only our farm but assisted John on his for several years clearing land, planting and harvesting crops until eventually, John decided to sell it. Because of his gratitude, he gave Father some land and his slave woman Pearl. Father was grateful for the land but he was reluctant to accept Pearl, not knowing how he might employ her or anything about her background. He accepted the offer, however and Pearl came to our farm.

Pearl's man, Jeremiah had died of a snake bite on John's farm a couple of months before she came to live with us. When Pearl arrived she didn't know that she was pregnant and her only child, Aliyah never knew her father.

After a short period of time, Pearl, a good natured and hard-working woman, seemed to fit in well with our family. We treated Pearl and Aliyah very kindly. Pearl seemed to be content living and working with us. She served mainly as the housekeeper, helping mother with household and other domestic chores such as washing, sewing, mending clothes and helping to keep the house livable. She also helped every morning milking the cows, feeding the chickens and collecting the eggs.

As Aliyah grew older, she helped us with other chores such as clearing land, planting and harvesting. She was a strong young woman and even tempered. She was always there working beside us during those long days that farm life required.

Pearl and Aliyah were an important part of our farm. We were grateful for their presence and considered them to be members of our family. It seemed to be a suitable arrangement that was working for all of us.

Chapter 4

In the summer of 1854, my brother Daniel was sixteen, active, adventurous and a healthy young male. When he went down to the river, Aliyah, fifteen, was usually with him. I was two years younger than Daniel but he'd usually let me tag along.

"Micah, are you coming?" he would ask, waving his arm toward me without saying much else. With his brief invitation, I would usually run and catch up with them.

The Altamaha River was our escape from the long hours working on the farm and the hot and humid Georgia summers. The slow moving water was cool and refreshing even in July. We were usually there in the late afternoon, staying for a few hours or until it began to get dark. It was normal for us to be walking back toward the farmhouse in total darkness.

We went to the river to swim or just to sit on the bank, relax and read a book. Often when I was casually fishing and reading a book in the shade of a large tree, Daniel and Aliyah would be frolicking in the water by the riverbank. When it was really hot, we would wade into the shallow water's edge and swim or just flop around to cool off. Sometimes we would swing out on a rope tied to a large tree limb and then drop into the water with a huge splash.

"Hey, watch what you're doing buddy. You'd better not get us wet," Daniel would yell at me, if the water sprayed too closely to where Aliyah and he were sitting.

Daniel was tall and muscular for his age, though somewhat wiry. His body was always richly tanned and he had blond hair that stood up when it got wet. He was a strong swimmer, gliding through the water easily. Sometimes when he would swim out away from the bank, I would yell jokingly, "Daniel, watch out for those big gators on the other side."

"Don't worry, I can out-swim any gator in this river," he replied, though he never had to prove it. We did see gators sometimes but they mostly ignored us. I guess they were trying to stay cool just like we were. We were smart enough however, to try to avoid them.

Aliyah was pretty and fun to be around. She always seemed to be happy no matter what we were doing. She joined our activities whether they were work or play.

"Aliyah, you're always smiling?" I would often say to her.

"Yeah, cause I like to," she'd reply with a big grin.

Aliyah was tall, slender and muscular. Even though I was a young teenager, I noticed that when she ran through the fields that the muscles in her legs rippled. She had a light brown complexion and black bushy hair. Her eyes were big and dark brown. Her smile was always soft and friendly. She usually talked in a low voice but could yell with a powerful voice if she were at the far end of a field.

I never saw Aliyah angry in all the time I was around her. Her temperament was easy going and she seemed to have a quiet confidence in herself. She also was a prankster. You always had to be on your guard when around her because you never knew when she would splash you with cold water or throw you a big mud pie. Aliyah was healthy too. She seemed to somehow avoid the minor coughs and colds that I would get every few months.

As I watched them play together in the water one day, they reminded me of young water birds, splashing around, having fun, unaware of their surroundings and totally enjoying themselves.

At first I thought it was just a big brother, little sister thing between Daniel and Aliyah. We were always together, whether working in the fields, playing in the river or eating meals, so I didn't notice anything different about their relationship. In fact, it was unusual when she wasn't with us. Through it all, Aliyah never complained about the hardest task or the messiest chore. If something had to be done, she did it without question.

As time went on though, I could see that their relationship was becoming something more. They were no longer just friends. They were getting closer with each other. I could see and feel it when I was around them. It was becoming uncomfortable for me. It was the little ways in which they looked at each other, worked and played together and smiled and teased each other.

"Mister Daniel, save me, I'm drowning," Aliyah would yell to Daniel as they played near the river.

"I'm coming, I'm coming" he'd reply. He would then dive in and swim over to her. She pretended to be going under the water and he would grab her and lift her up.

"Thank you, thank you. Oh, thank you for saving me Mister Daniel," she would say. Daniel would then give her a hug and swim away. While reading my book one day, out of the corner of my eye, I watched as they repeated this several times within an hour. It seemed to be a playful game. The routine was always the same. They didn't seem to notice me at all, nor did they seem to care.

As we left the river and walked back to the farm that day, I could see that Daniel and Aliyah were unconcerned with their differences in color and culture. Why should they care? They were having fun and enjoying their time with each other. What else could possibly matter?

I didn't feel that their relationship was right but Daniel was my big brother. He and Aliyah seemed to be happy. What could possibly be wrong with that?

Chapter 5

As the weeks went by, Daniel and Aliyah became more open in their behavior when around each other. There was a closeness, an intimacy that I hadn't seen before. While doing their chores, I noticed the casual looks, the secret smiles and the joking and subdued laughter. Regrettably, I wasn't asked to go down to the river with them as I had in the past. I was no longer the little brother just tagging along. I was something else now--an intruder in their daily activities.

Sometimes we would even argue about it. "Where do you think you're going Micah?"

"I'm going down to the river."

"You weren't invited. Must you always go where I go?"

"You mean you and Aliyah don't you?"

"That's right, and you should mind your own business."

"You'd better be careful Daniel. There could be trouble with what you're doing."

"Micah, you let me worry about that, okay?"

During this period in Antebellum Georgia, not only was racial intermarriage illegal but it was also against the law to teach a Negro to read. I knew that father and the local folks would not be happy with this blossoming relationship. I suspected it would be serious trouble for them if it continued.

I tried to abide by Daniel's wishes however. Whenever he went down to the river, I would usually wait a few minutes before departing and then go further down the riverbank. I loved to read by the flowing water and this was my special place too. I wasn't about to give it up.

One day, after completing our chores, surprisingly, Daniel asked, "Micah, do you want to go to the river with us?"

I looked at him quizzically, hesitated for a moment and then said, "Sure, why not?" I guess he felt sorry for me, for the things he had said a few weeks earlier. I ran into the house, grabbed a book and then left with them for the river.

We reached the spot on the river where we normally went. It was located near several large Sweetbay Magnolia trees with their creamy-white blooms and protective shade. It was a warm humid day with a slight breeze--a typical July day in southern Georgia.

I was reading, Robinson Crusoe, which I had started a few days earlier. Our pastor knew that I liked to read and would occasionally loan books to me from his personal collection. It was a point in the chapter where Crusoe was rescuing Friday from the Carib cannibals. I was sitting on the riverbank about one hundred feet away. Daniel was reading to Aliyah from the Bible. I could barely hear them talk, though I wouldn't admit to eavesdropping on their conversation. He was reading from the Book of Genesis, where God is talking to Abraham and telling him to take his only son Isaac, whom Abraham loved very much, to the land of Moriah and sacrifice him there as a burnt offering upon one of the mountains. Daniel would often read from the Bible to Aliyah and she seemed to enjoy listening to him read. He would talk in a deep voice at a passage where God was speaking.

Aliyah looked surprised by what Daniel had just read and asked, "Why would God ask Abraham to kill his only son?"

"God's testing him," Daniel replied. He wants to see if Abraham will do as he's commanded."

After we had been there for about half an hour, three teenage boys unexpectedly came upon us. One of the boys, Jeb Thomas, I had seen before at the farmers market. He seemed to be a very serious-minded, tough-looking fellow. He stood out from the others being tall and muscular, with ruddy blond hair and cornflower blue eyes. It seemed to me that he didn't smile very often and if he did, it was probably at someone else's expense.

The three boys, who looked to be about Daniel's age, approached the spot where Daniel and Aliyah were sitting. I knew they were from farms several miles west of ours. I had never talked with them, except to offer an occasional hello or give them a nod of the head when I saw them at church, which wasn't very often. They were carrying fishing poles and seemed to be scouting locations along the river where the fish might be biting.

Jeb walked up to where Daniel and Aliyah were sitting, looked at them oddly and then asked Daniel, "What do you think you're doing?"

"None of your damn business!" was Daniel's blunt and quick reply. Daniel was never one to run from trouble, so I knew where this was heading.

Jeb then said in a low, sarcastic tone, "It seems to me you're reading to that Negro girl," and then pointed his right middle finger close to Aliyah's face. At that point, Daniel sprang to his feet and gave Jeb a powerful shove that thrust Jeb flat on his back, into the shallow edge of the river. Jeb got up slowly, wiped himself off, looked up at Daniel with a half-hearted smile and then charged at him with all the speed and force he could muster. Soon, legs, arms and fists were flying in all directions.

I ran over to where they were fighting. They struggled fiercely as the rest of us stood by, watching and cheering on our champions. "Hit him Daniel," I yelled. "Hit him again."

After several minutes of violent physical activity--rolling around, throwing punches, kicking, grunting and yelling at each other, the affair ended. Jeb and Daniel were both totally exhausted from their physical contest and the exacting toll of the summer heat. They both seemed to collapse at about the same time, several feet apart from each other.

Luckily, neither seemed to have much bodily harm from their brawl. Only minor cuts and bruises were visible but both were filthy, covered in dirt and sweat.

Jeb got up slowly, picked up his pole and said to his friends, "Let's go." With that, the boys walked away as quickly as they had arrived.

Daniel got up, brushed himself off and then he and Aliyah grabbed their things and started walking back toward the farm. Aliyah was massaging Daniel's tired arm and shoulder muscles vigorously and was whispering in his ear as they walked. I followed them but I was about fifty feet behind.

I'm not certain if a consensus was reached that day on who was "King of the Altamaha" because the battle seemed to have ended in a draw. I do think however, that Daniel and Jeb earned a mutual respect for one another. It's interesting to look back now and realize that in a few short years fate would bring them both together again, fighting not against but alongside each other.

Chapter 6

A few days later, I decided to take my book and go down to the river and read peacefully in the shade. It was around four o'clock in the afternoon on another hot and humid day. We had finished our chores earlier, so I decided to make my escape.

I was walking alone near the river, when I spotted something moving in the brush. I thought it might be a small animal, maybe a deer so I moved quietly and carefully for a closer look. I've seen deer by the river many times before but not usually at this time of day. They were usually spotted early in the morning or later in the afternoon around dusk. To see one now would be surprising and exciting.

As I walked along slowly, I was careful not to make any noise not wanting to scare the deer. It was then that I saw something that I didn't expect to see. Remaining completely still, I saw Daniel and Aliyah lying together, embracing and kissing each other. I also heard their laughter. Startled by what I was seeing, I froze. I didn't know what to do.

"Stop it Daniel," I heard Aliyah say. She laughed and a moment later, laughed again. I remained motionless for a few moments. Embarrassed by my predicament, I slowly began to back away. After a few more slow steps backward, I turned and ran back toward our farmhouse, not knowing that I had dropped my Robinson Crusoe along the trail.

About an hour later, Daniel came into our room. I saw my book in his hand. "Is this yours?" he asked.

I looked up slowly, not wanting to look him directly in the eyes. I was afraid of what I would see. The book was in his hand and I said in a low voice, "Yes, it's mine."

"What else did you see Micah?"

"Nothing, I didn't see anything else."

"Nothing?"

I paused, took a deep breath and said, "Yes Daniel, I saw you and Aliyah, together."

"You cannot tell father," he said to me forcefully and with troubled eyes.

"I know."

He turned and slowly walked away from me. I was trembling, burdened with this new information, not knowing what to do with it, what to think or the thought of what father might do if he found out. I sensed that what I had seen was wrong but I wasn't sure why or how to react.

Several weeks later, in the early evening, I was walking toward the barn to check on the chickens when I heard father shouting at Daniel from inside the barn. He was sternly lecturing Daniel in a very loud voice.

"This can't continue. You and Aliyah cannot be together. She's not your race. She's not your kind. She's not one of us. The Bible forbids it. I forbid it. It has to end and it has to end now, Daniel. I forbid you to ever be with Aliyah again. Do you understand? Do you understand, Daniel?"

"Yes," Daniel replied. "I understand."

"I forbid you to be alone with her again," father said angrily, smashing a tool against the wall of the barn and quickly walking out and back toward the house. I hid behind a barrel so he couldn't see me.

A few moments later, I saw Daniel walking slowly out of the barn. He was hunched over with his head down. From the way he walked, you would have thought that father had just beaten him with a stick; but I knew he hadn't. I could see that father's ultimatum had crushed him. I felt very sorry for him. I had pity for him. He looked so unhappy, so down and alone. He caught a glimpse of me from the corner of his eye but kept walking. He didn't look at me. I knew he didn't want to talk now and I wasn't going to follow him.

Later, as I returned to the house, I wondered if it would be over now. Would this be the end of Daniel and Aliyah's relationship? Daniel usually did what he chose to do. Would he obey father now? I wondered if this really was the end.

Chapter 7

The Altamaha River gently winds more than one hundred and thirty miles from its northernmost point to the Atlantic Ocean. Its basin lies entirely within the state of Georgia. It is formed by the confluence of the Ocmulgee and Oconee rivers, approximately ninety miles west of Savannah. The Ohoopee River joins it further downstream. It flows toward the southeast and empties into the ocean just north of Brunswick.

Prior to and during the 19th century, flatboats and riverboats had used the Altamaha to reach inland towns and plantations. It was a major water route from the Atlantic coast to middle Georgia.

The River is home to a wide variety of plants, animals and fishes. Shortnose and Atlantic Sturgeons, the West Indian Manatee and the American Alligator live in the river's waters as well as otters, beavers and a large variety of other wildlife including frogs, turtles and snakes. The Altamaha delta is a stopover point for many species of migratory birds. Many trees such as the Long Leaf Pine, the Sweet Bay Magnolia and the Wax Myrtle are common along its shores.

The Indians used the Altamaha for transportation and fishing and had trails and settlements on both sides of the river. Its name comes from the Yamasee Indian chief, Altamaha. Indian populations in Georgia, consisting mostly of the Creek Indians up until the 16th century and later the Cherokee, were largely absent by the 1840's, due to fighting between the tribes and governmental policies of the Jackson Administration and the State of Georgia. Indian removal programs, during the late 1830's, were both harsh and unfair to the native Indians and resulted in much pain and suffering for them.

The Boden family had lived in the same area since about 1814. We originally settled here when my grandmother, Estella moved to the area following the death of my grandfather, Ira in one of the earlier Indian wars. Estella heard there was good, cheap land available for farming near Savannah. Being an adventurous, pioneering woman she migrated to the area just southwest of Savannah with her two young sons.

Estella traveled southeast from Tennessee with my father and Uncle Elijah and several other families who also made the journey. We were simple farmers, providing for our needs by the fruits of our labor and the good will of God and nature. We were able to survive by a willingness to learn farming, overcoming sometimes severe obstacles and a strong work ethic. We weren't much different from other hard-working families who had settled in the region.

I remember Granny Estella, yelling almost every morning at daybreak, "Get up, get up, we've got a lot of work to do today children. We have to milk the cows, feed the chickens, collect the eggs and work the land. Get up now and come have some breakfast." I knew that included my favorite--good cornbread and molasses.

Granny was a big woman in heart and size and very loving of her grandchildren. She was a strong woman both physically and mentally as was necessary in those rugged days. She was the foundation of our family for the decades and generations that followed.

Chapter 8

There were two events occurring in 1854 that profoundly affected our family. The first was a yellow fever epidemic that hit Savannah and the surrounding areas, killing about one-thousand souls and bringing devastating grief to many families in the area.

"I feel sick mother," I remember my younger brother Thomas saying one evening after dinner. He hadn't eaten much that evening which was unusual for him. Later that night he developed a high fever, was vomiting and had severe neck and back pain.

"He's very sick and seems to be getting worse," Pearl told my mother. "Let's try to cool him off with wet rags." He continued to worsen throughout the night and the next morning seemed to be delirious. His skin became jaundiced and then he went into a coma. A few days later, he was gone.

"Why have you taken our son, dear lord?" I heard mother saying tearfully as she prayed. "Why did you have to take him now? He was so young and such a good boy. We loved him so much." Mother was devastated. She cried daily. Her grief seemed to last for months. He was her youngest child and was only five. Mother felt guilty because she had tried so hard, prayed so much to make him well, but couldn't do anything to prevent his death. It was something she couldn't understand.

Mother never was herself again after the loss of Thomas. It was as if someone had ripped a part of her heart away. Father was also shaken by his death but seemed better able to cope with it. We all tried to comfort her in the weeks and months that followed but to no avail. Her deep despondency lasted for many years.

For Daniel and me, it was the loss of our little buddy. When we went fishing, he would tag along. If we were working on the barn roof, he wanted to be up there with us. Losing Thomas was very painful for all of us and the pain and memories stayed with us long after his death.

The second event that year, a hurricane, caught us totally without warning. It was early September and father, Daniel, Aliyah and I were out harvesting vegetables when we noticed the skies darkening and the wind beginning to pick up. We had some light showers earlier in the morning but we didn't think much of it. It was summer and we were accustomed to showers and thunderstorms that could roll in anytime, day or night.

"The sky is darkening and the wind is starting to blow really hard," father said. "Hurry up and get back to the house before this storm gets worse and it starts to lightning."

"We need to get the animals to safety," Daniel yelled back.

"Daniel, go find the horse and cows and bring them back to the barn. Aliyah, make sure the chickens are in the shed. Micah, go find your mother and Pearl and tell them to get into the house quickly," father directed.

"I hope they're close by and not down by the stream," I replied.

We did as father said and then went into the house. We had just finished closing all the windows and securing the doors as the winds got even stronger. I could hear limbs, in nearby trees, snapping and then crashing to the ground.

"I've never seen anything like this. Get away from the windows," father said, with fear in his eyes.

The winds began to blow very hard and were howling, horribly. We continued to hear loud cracking sounds from outside the house and knew that trees were falling. I could hear the structure of the house moaning and the doors and windows straining with each breath of wind from the powerful storm. We worried that our house could not stand up to its fury. It continued to blow its strong winds and pounding rain on our house for hours. Water was leaking from the roof in every room. The storm went on and on. We prayed for it to end.

Later that evening, the winds subsided and curiously, we decided it was safe to go out and look around. We were surprised. Our house and land looked much different than it had the day before. Large trees were lying on their sides all around the house, including one of the large pecan trees.

Everywhere you looked there was wind damage. The roof had lost most of its wooden shingles. Several sections of fences were either knocked down or missing entirely--strong winds having carried them away to places unknown.

"Father, look at the barn. The roof is gone," Daniel said.

"Check on the animals. Make sure they're safe," he replied.

We looked inside the barn but the animals were missing. The door of the barn had blown off and we assumed the animals had run off, having been frightened by the storm.

"Oh my," father said. "Daniel, you and Micah go to the fields and see if you can find the animals. I'll go down by the stream and take a look."

It took us several hours but we did find most of the animals. The cows seemed to be spooked but were okay. Unfortunately, we found about twenty of the chickens lying dead on the ground. They must have been scared by the storm and thrown about by its winds.

"The fields are a mess. We'll have to see if we can save any of the corn," father said. The cotton fields had also taken a beating. Many of the plants and vegetables that weren't damaged by the wind were crushed or flooded by the pounding rains.

It took several months to make repairs to the house and barn and to clean up our fields. We heard later that a hurricane had come ashore near the Florida-Georgia border and had caused severe damage all along the coastline including many homes and buildings in Savannah.

That year was one that wouldn't soon be forgotten. The tragedy of losing our brother Thomas and the devastating hurricane, had a lasting impact that affected all of us for the rest of our lives.

Chapter 9

Though he never spoke of it, father had seen the growing relationship between Daniel and Aliyah and felt that he needed to act. He decided that the best solution was to send Aliyah to live with a farmer about five miles down the road from us.

Aaron and his wife Eula had two daughters who were about the same age as Daniel and me and a younger son. Aaron was a good man, kind and religious and my father knew he would treat Aliyah well. His farm was about the same size as ours. Father knew Aaron from the church and they occasionally worked together when taking their produce to the market in Savannah. They were there to help each other in time of need and had done so several times in the past.

Father felt that if he could separate Daniel and Aliyah by some distance, it would make it difficult for them to be together. His decision caused divisiveness and considerable hurt within our family for many months. Pearl objected at first to the move because she didn't want to be apart from her daughter.

"Why are you doing this to us, Mister Jacob?" Pearl asked father. "Why must you do this? We do our work every day, without complaint. We're part of your family. It's not right to separate family."

"I'm doing it because I have to, Pearl. There's no other way. It's not right for them to be together as much as they are now. Their relationship can't continue this way. They can't be together any longer. It's sinful. You have to understand that."

Mother even argued against it, feeling it was wrong to separate Aliyah from her mother. "Why not talk with them Jacob? I'm sure you can reason with them if you'll just try to talk to them. Why must we send Aliyah away? We need her here. She's part of our family. She belongs here. We love Aliyah like one of our own. You know that."

"I'm sorry Sarah. I care for Aliyah as much as you do but we have to end this relationship now. They won't stop seeing each other on their own. We must separate them. I've talked with Aaron and he's willing to let Aliyah live and work on his farm. He will be good to her. He will treat her as he would one of his own. I know he will. He's a good man."

Although it took several months to get over it, I think that both Pearl and mother came to realize that moving Aliyah was probably the best thing to do, although it was painful for everyone.

"You can visit Aliyah every week if you want," father said to Pearl. "I'll even take you there in the wagon with me when I go to see Aaron. It's really the best thing for both of them."

"You'll let me visit her every week?"

"Yes Pearl, you can, as long as it doesn't interfere with your chores around here."

To both Aliyah and Daniel, it must have seemed like the end of the world. Both became very quiet and subdued until the day Aliyah left with father to go to Aaron's farm.

I remember Aliyah saying goodbye to each of us, then slowly, climbing into the wagon. As she sat down, she put her head down and didn't look up again. As father drove away, there wasn't a dry eye amongst us.

The wagon made the turn around the bend and slowly disappeared in the distance. I had a deep, sick feeling in my stomach. It was gloomy for all of us that day and for several weeks thereafter. We would all miss her and her lovely smile, very much.

It took us months to adjust to Aliyah leaving. I don't think Daniel ever did.

Pearl missed Aliyah and would walk to Aaron's farm to see her almost every week or as often as she could. It wasn't an easy trip by foot. It usually took Pearl an hour or more each way depending on the conditions of the road. When it rained, the roads were muddy and walking was difficult. During dry spells, the dust was so bad that it made seeing and breathing quite challenging. I remember seeing Pearl covering her face with a piece of cloth to protect her face from the dust.

The severe heat also made the trip a summer hardship. Depending on the temperature, several stops along the way to rest in the shade, escape from the glaring sun or for a cool drink of water from a running stream, were usually necessary.

Sometimes, father would need to visit Aaron. He would take the wagon and mule, which made the journey a little easier for Pearl. She usually sat up front, next to him. He made the trip about once a month. His visits were usually to assist Aaron with clearing, planting, harvesting or to borrow tools. Sometimes they would share seed for planting. By helping each other, they were able to accomplish more during the growing season.

I don't think Daniel ever forgave my father for sending Aliyah away. Over time, Daniel became quite somber in mood. He would go down to the river by himself and sit quietly for hours. I could tell he still had deep feelings for Aliyah and I knew this pain would be with him for a long time.

With Aliyah gone, there was more work for Daniel and me. I also missed the fun and cheerfulness that Aliyah brought by just being around. She had never complained and had always been willing to help. I really did miss her.

I can't say that Daniel never saw Aliyah again. I had heard from a friend that he had seen them meeting secretly on occasion. However, the meetings were much less frequent now and I never saw them together again until after the war.

As time went on, I knew that father was content with his decision and Daniel continued to be quiet and aloof. Being Daniel's brother, I could discuss almost anything with him but I couldn't mention the name, Aliyah. On those few occasions that I did mention her, he would look at me with a sharp glare and then turn and walk away without saying a word.

Over the next few years, our farm grew as we expanded our acreage, mostly by growing more cotton. But our world was heading into a very dark period. Our family didn't discuss it much even though we had heard rumors that Georgia would secede from the Union if South Carolina did.

I still remember father praying for peace and goodwill at every meal. I remember his words as if it were yesterday. He seemed to sense that war was an evil unleashed and that our Country was moving too quickly toward it. "Please Dear Lord, have our leaders show patience and wisdom before deciding on secession. There's a dark cloud coming our way that's for sure. Please give them the wisdom to think clearly during this time of peril and do what is right. War is an awful scourge that is on our doorstep and is about to be released. Please Lord we ask for your protection from this approaching storm. Amen."

The day we heard that South Carolina had fired upon Fort Sumter, was a day of sadness in our home. Daniel and I had grown up with some awareness of slavery, but it seemed a small part of our day-to-day lives. Our relationship with Pearl and Aliyah had always been a good one and both families seemed to benefit from that relationship. Perhaps that was naïve thinking, but Pearl and Aliyah had always been around, working with us on the farm and we considered them to be family. We were always taught to respect them from a young age. But there were large plantations in Georgia and much of the South where shocking abuses were taking place. How long would the culture of slavery be allowed to continue?

The Country had been slowly drifting toward a necessary resolution of the slavery question for decades. The final settlement had always been pushed forward to a time in the future. But President Lincoln had been elected and the time for a solution had arrived even though its final cost was unknown. Our family didn't want war and looking back now, we really didn't understand what total war meant. It was coming however, and there was nothing we could do to stop it.

Chapter 10

In the summer of 1862, the Confederacy called for additional volunteers to fight the war. At the time of secession there was jubilation and enthusiasm all across the South. Young men came forward in droves volunteering to protect their homeland. Daniel and I had tried to join in the previous year but the army wouldn't take us due to a shortage of weapons and equipment. But the war was lasting longer than most had expected. As the deaths and casualties continued to mount, the exhilaration and motivation to join and fight had tempered significantly. Volunteers weren't coming forward as readily as they had in the past and the shortage of soldiers was now taking a toll on units within the army.

In April of 1862, the Confederate government passed its first draft law, about a year before the federal government did. It was unpopular in the South. Until it was abolished in December, 1863 rich men who were drafted could hire substitutes. The law also allowed exemptions for important positions on the home front such as civil officials, railroad and river workers, telegraph operators, teachers and druggists. The law was amended again later to allow exemption for those who owned more than twenty slaves.

"This is a rich man's war being fought by poor farm boys," father said. "Most of us don't even own slaves or at least very few. We're fighting this war to protect the rich man's right to own hundreds of slaves to work his large plantations. It's just not right. It's an immoral war under the eyes of God."

As the war dragged on, it was showing its awful face. We had already had a number of local boys killed due to the fierce fighting and disease. Others had returned home with shocking disabilities such as lost hands, feet, arms and legs and some with gross disfigurement. Those who returned talked of the awful carnage they had seen--the death of hundreds, even thousands of young men and the senseless destruction of animals and property. It made a big impression on those of us who were still at home.

Being aware of father's views on the war, Daniel and I decided to talk with mother and father anyway. We wanted go get their approval for our desire to volunteer. We knew however, that they would be very much opposed to our joining. "No, we don't approve of it. You can't go," mother said. "You've heard your father. This is an awful war. So many good boys have already died and for what? We can't lose you. We won't let you go."

"We need you here on the farm more than Jeb Davis needs you in his army," father said. "What are they fighting for anyway? The South cannot win this war. They have more of everything up north: people, railroads and manufacturing. Our boys are just marching off to die. We don't want you to go. You have to stay home. You're needed here."

"Father, the South has been invaded. We have to defend it. There's even conscription now because they can't get enough volunteers. They're going to come and find us anyway." I paused for a moment then said, "Daniel and I have discussed this father and we've decided to join. It's something we have to do."

Father looked at Daniel and then turned back to me. "Is this how you really feel? Is there nothing more I can say on the matter to convince you to stay?"

"No father. It's something we have to do. We're going to leave in a few days. Don't worry, we'll end this war quickly so we can come home and get back to farming," I said, with a half-smile. "We'll end it and then come home. I promise."

"I'm so worried you boys won't return. What about the boys we've seen at church, the one without an arm, the other without a leg? Little Billy Thompson got shot in the face." Mother then looked upward, "Please God, when will this war end?"

"Don't worry Mother. Daniel and I will look after each other. We'll keep each other out of danger. We'll win one or two big battles and then those Yanks will go running home. They won't want to fight us anymore. You'll see."

Mother and father finally consented a few days later. They didn't approve of our joining but said they wouldn't try to stop us. They said they understood why we felt the way we did. Maybe they were just saying that but it made our departure a little easier. Mother helped us pack, thinking of all the little things she knew we would forget. After losing our little brother, the thought of losing one or both of us was too hard for her to even imagine. I knew our absence would be especially tough on her.

We didn't know what was ahead of us or how it might end. We did know however, that we weren't joining the army to fight to preserve slavery. That wasn't an issue for Daniel and me. We felt strongly that since the Yankees had invaded the South, it was our duty to fight and defend Georgia and if necessary, die for her. But, we weren't about to say that in front of mother.

Chapter 11

We started on our journey to Savannah several days later. A friend of ours, Johnny Williams from a nearby farm, accompanied us on the trip. If we were lucky, we would hitch a ride on a wagon with a friendly farmer at least part of the way. Otherwise, we would walk.

Savannah was about fifty miles northeast of the farm and it would normally take a full day to walk it or two days if we stopped along the way. We had heard that the 54th Georgia Infantry Regiment was organizing there and needed volunteers. Others had gone before us and now it was time for us to do our duty too.

This wasn't our first trip to Savannah. We had gone with father several times before when he traveled to the farmer's market there. Usually, Daniel or I would travel with him to help unload the wagon or to load supplies we purchased.

Savannah was the first city of Georgia and it was the thirteenth and final colony in America, founded in 1733. It was a planned city, laid out in a series of grids with public parks and squares. Savannah had flourished prior to the war and was considered one of the most beautiful cities in America. It was a city built on a bluff beside the Savannah River and noted for its great oak trees and lovely architecture.

The war greatly changed things however. The sea blockades by the Union Navy had largely strangled the economy of the city. Effects of the war were visible everywhere including shortages of food and other day-to-day living supplies. The shortage of coffee was causing the locals to do without or use other ingredients such as roasted grains or peanuts. Without sugar, residents were turning to molasses to make their cakes and cookies. They were forced to make do with what they had and use their resourcefulness to find suitable substitutes.

We arrived at the recruiting station early in the morning. It appeared to have been an abandoned warehouse or perhaps an old hardware store converted for its new purpose. The building maintained a rich unidentified smell clearly suggesting an earlier use that was a challenge for our nostrils.

Standing outside by the entrance having a smoke was the officer in charge, Captain William Edwards. He pointed us to the door and then followed us inside. He was a short, balding fellow, somewhat rotund with a deep voice. He appeared to be in his late thirties or early forties.

As we walked inside, we heard his booming voice from behind. "Welcome gentleman, get in line over there." It wasn't a long line he pointed to, as only a few others were standing there. It seemed we were waiting in line for something that was about to happen.

After standing there patiently for about twenty minutes, a doctor came into the building and then called us over, one-by-one, for an examination. He quickly checked our eyes, ears, mouths and limbs and pronounced us medically cleared. I didn't see anyone fail his exam that day which reinforced my opinion that the need for soldiers was great.

We were then instructed to see a sergeant on the opposite side of the room. There, he directed us to put our signatures on the enlistment papers he placed in front of us. This action officially mustered us in to the 54th Georgia.

At that moment, Daniel and I felt very proud. We were doing our duty for Georgia, protecting our homes from the belligerent invaders from the north. We signed-up for three years or the duration of the war, whichever occurred first. They then paid us the handsome sum of fifty dollars each. That was easily the most money I ever had at one time.

"We're soldiers now Daniel. I'm ready for a fight."

"No need to rush it, little brother. The war will find us soon enough. You can count on that," Daniel replied.

Mother had taught Daniel and me to read and write, though we weren't considered well-educated by common standards. We had spent a few years attending our local schoolhouse but I improved my education mostly by reading whatever I could find. I would read books I'd find at the country store, at church or by trading with friends who also liked to read. However, compared to most of the soldiers in our company, Daniel and I were more educated. Most of them were poor farm boys who could barely read or write. Some of us said we enlisted because it was our duty, others for the adventure but all of us surely enjoyed getting paid that day.

As time passed, whenever policies or directives would come down from headquarters and if our Lieutenant wasn't present, the Captain would usually ask me to read it to the other soldiers. He would then comment afterwards on its substance. I also read newspapers or magazines to the group that occasionally found their way to our unit or fellow soldiers. I didn't mind this extra chore since it kept us informed of current news and ensured that we were aware of any new regulations coming our way.

It was a surprise to see Jeb Thomas there that same day. Was it a coincidence, I wondered? Jeb was the boy that Daniel had fought, several years earlier on the banks of the Altamaha. We hadn't seen him much since then but it was good to see him now. He was a new private, just like us in the 54th.

Jeb and Daniel saw each other, gave each other a quick nod of the head and that was about it. I thought it somewhat ironic that these two former combatants were now fighting on the same side. I also knew that if there was a fight coming, I wanted to stay close to both of them.

Chapter 12

We were now part of an infantry company, Company B, which would normally have about one hundred men. It was commanded by Captain William Peters. Our regiment, the 54th Georgia Infantry, had ten companies and was commanded by Colonel Joshua Judges. Although unknown to us at the time, this would be our home for the next three years.

"You new volunteers, line up outside with the rest of the company," I heard one of the sergeants yell. With that, we hurried outside to the front of the building. Our unit, which we hadn't seen in formation previously, was now gathering outside. I hurried to get in line but I noticed that my fellow soldiers looked very similar to me--mostly young farm boys with great anxiety about what lay ahead.

"Good afternoon, men. For you new recruits, I'm Captain Peters, your company commander." He was a tall slender man, who looked to be in his mid-thirties. He had bushy, red hair and a weather beaten look, probably from plowing fields under a hot southern sun, I thought.

"Uniforms and weapons are scarce right now gentleman but you'll have them soon enough," Captain Peters said. Daniel and I hadn't really brought much with us from home, so we were looking forward to receiving new uniforms. "The clothes on your backs will be your uniforms for now." He paused, looked around slowly at all of us and then said, "The pay will be good. You'll receive $11 a month as a private. I bet most of you farm boys don't see that much in three months."

"And, if we're lucky, we'll be paid every four months," said a soldier standing next to me, with his hand over his mouth and spoken quietly. He was wearing a soiled, worn gray uniform and had shoes with holes in them. He had been here for a while, I reasoned.

The first few days and weeks in camp were routine and boring. During the day we would drill, drill and then drill some more. Usually, this went on until sundown. We didn't have our muskets yet, so we drilled with wooden sticks that vaguely looked like muskets. The biggest dangers we faced now were getting splinters in our hands and blisters on our feet.

Our daily routine was announced by drums. Reveille was sounded at five in the morning, followed by morning roll call, breakfast call and sick call. After that were assemblies for guard duty, drill or to begin our marches.

Every day we practiced drills that our company would be using while marching in formation and maneuvering in battle. The drilling was repetitious but we understood its necessity. The reasoning being, if we repeated these drills and formations enough times, it would sink in and become routine, enabling us to correctly respond to verbal commands at the critical moments. The only drilling I remembered at home was my father teaching me as a young boy how to milk a cow and cast a fishing line. Even then, it took many repetitions to get it right.

During those evenings when we weren't totally exhausted from the day's activities, we would sit around the campfire discussing politics and religion, singing and playing cards. We also told stories of our hometowns and the loved ones we had left behind. Occasionally we would get to our fishing stories and it was always worth the wait to see who had the taller tale. We were all fond of fishing so that was a common discussion amongst us.

"I once caught a sturgeon in the Altamaha that was six feet long," said our friend, Johnny Williams, sitting around the campfire holding out his arms trying to demonstrate his point. Upon hearing this, it got very quiet and everyone looked at each other then back at Johnny.

"That's true. I've heard tales of even larger ones being caught," said Daniel. "They can weigh over two hundred pounds."
Everyone was surprised by his comment but seemed to accept Daniel as an authority on the subject.

Being in camp, gave us plenty of time to observe each other and what kind of soldiers and people we were. I remember one soldier, in particular, a Private Billy Dale, who was in our Company. Billy was a short fellow with curly brown hair. His build was thin but wiry. His voice had an annoying nasal tone about it and even more so when he got excited. I never really liked him and I don't think many in our Company did. He was a bit odd and seemed to have a mean streak in him that I didn't see in the other soldiers. During later months, when we were sitting around in camp, he would occasionally shoot at birds, squirrels and other small animals just for fun. It seemed to give him a strange pleasure when he could kill something. Several times he was reprimanded by our Sergeant for wasting ammunition.

He also had a perverted tendency to search the belongings of fallen enemy soldiers rather than treating their bodies with the respect I felt they deserved. That fact about him was especially annoying to me and I let him know it on several occasions as did others.

"My God Billy, what are you doing? Show some respect, will you?" I said to him following one of our skirmishes in '63, when I saw him picking over the belongings of a dead soldier.

"Why should I? They're dead. They don't need that stuff anymore do they, Micah?" he said with a distorted grin.

"Their families may. Show some respect, that's all I'm asking. Will you please?"

"How about if you mind your damn business Micah and I'll mind mine," he replied.

One evening, I was talking with several soldiers around the camp fire after a long day of drilling. We were discussing how we might react when facing the enemy for the first time. "I hope I can pull the trigger when the time comes," I said. "I just pray that I won't be shaking so badly that I can't fire. I've heard tales of soldiers being so nervous in battle that they repeatedly loaded their musket without firing one shot. I hope that's not me."

Billy, who was walking close by overheard me and said, "Don't worry. Killing Yankees will be as easy as killing squirrels in your backyard. And, I hope I get to kill plenty of them. God knows this is a wonderful opportunity that I don't want to miss."

"But aren't you going to feel a little different about killing humans rather than squirrels?" I asked him. "The Bible says thou shall not kill."

"I don't care what the Bible says. I'm going to kill as many of them as the good Lord will let me," Billy said.

I looked at him in disbelief, then got up and walked away. I was hoping that Billy was just making big talk in front of us and was a little more human than that but I had my doubts.

We had soldiers in our regiment from many Georgia counties including Appling, Barrow, Bartow, Chatham, Harris, Lamar and Muscogee. Most of us were young, under thirty, but our Company included soldiers of all ages from fifteen to sixty-two. Many of us had hunted wild pigs, deer, turkeys, raccoons and possums for food or skins. Others had fired muskets at targets just for fun. However, none of us had ever hunted or shot at other human beings.

The food at this time wasn't too bad because in addition to our rations, we would on occasion, get some good local cooking, including cakes and pies, from the appreciative residents of Savannah. They seemed to enjoy treating us to some tasty home cooking from time to time.

"Don't get too used to this good treatment boys," Captain Peters said to us one day. "It'll be changing as soon as we move out and join the rest of the regiment."

We usually had coffee with our meals though that was becoming harder to get for both us and the local citizens due to the Union naval blockade. Anything else we needed, we could get from local sutlers. Sutlers were civilians who when approved by the commanders hung around the camps and sold those items that weren't part of our normal rations or that were in short supply, such as needles, thread and candy. They operated mainly on a cash basis and they almost always overcharged but we were willing to pay for those little extras that we wanted. After a while, even the sutlers became hard to find.

I tried to write home as often as possible, to let the folks back there know what was going on. I tried to give them as much information as I could without giving them reason to worry. Rumors were abundant in camp so we never really knew for sure what was factual and what wasn't.

Receiving letters from home was always a great source of excitement in camp. Those who received letters were always very happy to get them and those who didn't were usually quiet and disappointed.

Hearing news from home was a way to stay in touch with family and friends and the connection to our past. Though mail would be sporadic later in the war, especially when the unit was moving, it was coming daily while we were in the Savannah area.

Letters could bring news of great joy and deep sadness. "I'm a father, I'm a father," I heard Private Terrell Anderson yell excitedly one day. He had just received a letter from home and found out that his new daughter was born a week earlier.

I also remember the day when Private Wayne Johnson received a letter from home and learned of his mother's passing. "I knew she was ill, but I didn't expect this to happen so soon. She got the fever and it never seemed to go away. She just kept getting sicker and weaker. She's with the Lord now."

Since I didn't have a girl back home, all of my letters were to mother and father. Daniel didn't write very often, so I did the writing for both of us. Before finishing the letter, I always checked with him to see if he wanted me to include any news.

Daniel seemed to be aloof much of the time while we were in camp. I assumed it was from boredom or homesickness. When I would say to Daniel, "Why don't you write a letter to mother?" he would just shrug his shoulders and look away. He didn't seem to want to talk much about what he was doing or thinking or to hear what was happening at home. I said in my letters that he was fine and kept busy drilling with the rest of us.

"It's been tough on the farm since you and Daniel left. We still haven't had much rain. Father says if we don't get rain soon, the crops will fare poorly this year," mother said, in a recent letter to me. That was the hardest part of being away from home--when there were problems there was little we could do about it. For that reason, Mother usually didn't mention bad news.

We finally got to train with a real weapon after about three weeks. It was an Enfield rifle musket that required muzzle loading. To get it ready to fire, took about twenty seconds. Samuel Walker, our platoon sergeant said, "If you get good boys, you may be able to fire three times within a minute. This is especially important, if you ever want to be a grandfather." We knew exactly what he meant.

All soldiers in the Company took turns with the musket, practicing firing techniques. The bullet and powder were enclosed in a paper cartridge which the soldier had to open with his teeth. This usually resulted in a black mouth. He would then pour the powder into the rifle barrel, setting the bullet in the muzzle and pushing it down with a ramrod. He placed a percussion cap on the tube leading into the base of the barrel, pulled the hammer back or cocked it, aimed and fired. It took a total of 9-separate rifle actions in sequence to be able to fire the musket.

"If a soldier has good eyes and steady hands, he can hit a target four hundred yards away." After a short pause, Sergeant Walker said, "If you can see them, you'd better be able to shoot them, because they can see you too."

I knew that my life depended on my ability to handle the weapon, so I took this training very seriously. When we didn't have a real musket, we would practice using a replica or a stick. We practiced the techniques in the correct order and timing by talking ourselves through it with our fellow soldiers observing. It was essential that we learn these techniques and learn them well. We were all aware of this. We knew our lives would depend on each other and our ability to fire these weapons rapidly and accurately.

We practiced firing at targets that were set against a sandy hill at several distances. This gave us an indication as to who could and couldn't shoot well in the company. I got to be pretty good firing the musket but I wasn't as good as Daniel. He grasped the firing techniques very quickly and showed a real knack for all things military. This had surprised me, since he disliked the rigors and regimentation of daily farming.

Daniel was one of the most accurate shooters in the company. We had hunted together as teenagers but we didn't bring food home for the table very often. In camp, however, he picked things up better than others, especially the firing of the musket and the battle drills. After observing Daniel every day in camp, I was convinced that he was the one I would follow in a battle. He would take care of me, I thought. Of course, that's what big brothers are supposed to do. They look out for their little brothers.

I started to notice one troubling problem that continued throughout the war. The wearing of warm clothing in the summer heat was a boon for body lice. They would get on you, and it was difficult to get rid of them. Boiling your clothes in water or just picking them off, were the ways of dealing with them. Being in close proximity to other soldiers made it easy for them to spread and soon everyone was scratching with red blotches on the skin, especially around the folds on their bodies. Armpits and waist areas were very popular sites for lice.

Other annoying problems such as chiggers and mosquitoes kept us awake at night. Also, camps did a poor job of keeping latrines away from water sources which often lead to troublesome diseases such as dysentery. Other illnesses that took their toll on soldiers were pneumonia, measles, small pox and malaria.

We stayed in the Savannah area for several months and then one day we were told to get prepared to move out. For most of us this was good news because drilling all day and sitting around in camp at night was getting old. Some of us were even itching for a fight. I think I played more games of cards and told more tall tales during those few months we were in camp than I had in my previous twenty-two years. I too, was ready to go even though I didn't know where we were heading or what dangers we'd be facing.

"Micah, I hear we may be going to Charleston. No one is really saying but those are the rumors I'm hearing," said Charlie Reynolds, another new private, who I'd met only a few weeks earlier. Because we had a lot in common, we soon became good friends.

"I know. Since the firing on Fort Sumter, rumor is the Yankees want to attack Charleston Harbor and shut it down. There's a fight coming for us Charlie and that's for sure."

Chapter 13

"We're heading to Charleston," Lieutenant Robert Hill, our platoon leader said with excitement, as we were having breakfast one morning. "We'll be moving out in one hour. Hurry up, finish eating and then pack up."

I glanced at Daniel and said, "Can you imagine that? We're heading to Charleston, South Carolina, the place where this war started with the firing on Fort Sumter."

"Yeah, I wonder how they feel about that now?" he asked.

We rushed to finish our meal, packed our things and got ready for the move. We didn't know what we'd be facing in the weeks and months ahead but we looked at it with a mix of anxiety and excitement.

I anticipated a long, hot and dusty road march to Charleston so I was pleased when I found out we were going by rail. We marched from our camp over to the Charleston and Savannah Railroad and loaded our personal gear and company equipment. I'd never ridden on a train before, so it was exciting to be taking my first ride. Although the circumstances for this trip were not my first choice, I was still happy to be going. Daniel didn't say so but I could tell he was also. His eyes were wide open, looking in all directions and taking in the sights as we pulled slowly out of the station.

Savannah to Charleston is a little over a hundred miles but it took us about six hours by rail. The soldiers in our car were making humorous conversation during the trip but there was some concern expressed about what we might find when we got to Charleston. We had read in local papers that Union forces were making an offensive against Charleston and its harbor defenses, so that was the number one topic of discussion.

"I've read that Union gunboats can throw shells several miles. We're going to be in for a rough time of it in the next few weeks," said Private Edward Wilson, a fellow soldier from the Savannah area. Edward was a soldier who had joined our unit just before we departed for Charleston. I liked him. He also liked to read just like me but he could be gloomy at times, so I tried to avoid the deeper questions with him.

"They've got to find us first," said Private Jimmy Patterson, "and I intend to keep my head down and my body hidden. They can't shoot me if they can't see me," he said with a big grin. Jimmy was fun to be around. He always seemed to have a joke for the appropriate moment. Jimmy was tall and lanky and had straight red hair so we nicknamed him "scarecrow".

We arrived in Charleston during the late afternoon. After departing the train in an orderly fashion, we removed and secured our equipment. We were tired and cramped from riding in the train so it was a relief to get out, stretch our legs and walk around a little. Also, we needed some fresh air. Riding on a train in close quarters with your buddies and their body odors, going days without a bath was quite challenging to the nasal passages.

"Whew. That smelled like a pigpen in there," said Daniel, after he departed the train. "I don't think I'd have lasted another hour in there," pointing back toward the train.

"At least we're riding pigs and not walking pigs," I replied. "Sure does beat walking those dusty roads in this heat. I'll take this moving pig farm any day."

"Yeah, you're right about that Micah."

We picked up our equipment then marched a short distance away from the train station to an open field, where we made our camp for the evening. It was early summer so we knew what to expect--heat, maybe rain and mosquitoes. I had spent many of my first months in the army sleeping under a blanket or anything I could find, to escape the mosquitoes. The combination of heat, being under a blanket and the buzzing of mosquitoes made sleeping difficult even for a hardy sleeper such as me. Sometimes I was even the butt of jokes because of my sleeping habits. But that was my mosquito survival technique and it worked.

"You look like you're in a cocoon, Micah. Hell, the mosquitoes can't even find you," said Lieutenant Hill.

"Yea and he's so skinny, they wouldn't take more than one bite anyway," replied Private Patterson.

Anyway, I know that those were some of my longest nights in the army, trying to sleep between mosquito attacks and being soaked in perspiration from the summer heat. I wasn't sure at this point who were the greater enemies—the boys in blue or the buzzing mosquitoes looking for an open patch of my skin?

An hour after departing the train, we had our evening meal. It consisted of coffee, salt pork, hard bread, beans and dried peaches. We occasionally had pickles, dried fruits and fresh vegetables depending on the circumstances and what was in season. Sometimes desiccated vegetables were served to us. We were told that was to prevent scurvy.

The next day, we woke up at dawn, broke camp after breakfast and then gathered by our equipment and muskets. We always stacked our weapons in camp unless there was an immediate threat of danger. We formed into a four columns and began our march. Lieutenant Hill told us that we would be performing duty in the

Charleston area in support of the harbor defenses. We were moving to a place called Morris Island.

When I first saw Fort Wagner, I wasn't overly impressed. It was larger than I had expected with its built up parapets, the large mounds of dirt and supporting materials designed to protect soldiers from bullets, cannon fire and the arching naval shells but it didn't look like the forts or castles I had seen in books about Europe. It did have however, a moat surrounding it. The moat was there to slow down the attacking enemy and channel them into selected locations where they could be fired upon by weapons inside the fort. Having seen drawings of European castles though, I was a little disappointed.

But in spite of my notions about forts, I thought it looked formidable and secure. Our company rotated through several locations in and around the Island to include duty inside Fort Wagner. It seemed like it could withstand an attack, even a bombardment from the sea that we expected would be coming soon.

In June of 1863, activity started to pick up around the Island. We continued to improve our fortifications and dug or built new defensive positions as necessary.

"Dig those trenches deep and sturdy and with good cover from above. The enemy is going to attack us with infantry, gunboat fire and artillery," Lieutenant Hill said. The thought of being attacked from the air by an enemy that we couldn't even see, was a very sobering thought indeed.

When July came, we were glad for the time we had spent improving our positions. Union gunboats arrived and began to shell our fortifications both day and night. From the flashes in the distance and the sounds of the bombardments, it seemed like the firing was coming at us from all directions and in fact, it was.

This was the first time that any of us had been shot at, so anxiety and tensions were high. Not only that, but because the firing of the weapons occurred throughout the night, almost every night, we were severely tested as to our ability to get any sleep or rest. I remember praying on many occasions, asking God to make the gunboats leave so that we could at least get some rest. I hated using my prayers for such matters but after several days, the body and mind, without much sleep, gets fatigued and very testy.

Daniel and I pulled guard duty every few days, but not always at the same time. We were required to remain awake all night and look for anything suspicious on land or coming from the sea. On the nights when we had a full moon, this wasn't so difficult. But on the really dark or overcast nights, it was difficult to see anything. It was also very scary. Every little noise we heard was treated with suspicion. Most of the sounds we heard turned out to be small animals foraging for food but we never knew for sure.

We were warned that anyone caught sleeping on guard duty would be shot, so we were motivated to stay awake. I didn't know of anyone who had been shot for sleeping on guard duty but I had heard stories of some that had. I wasn't about to find out first hand if it was true or not but staying awake late at night was still quite a challenge.

The gunboats and their constant firing were taking a toll on us. It wasn't long afterward also, that artillery was positioned by Union forces across from us on Folly Island. This significantly increased the amount of incoming fire we received on all of our positions throughout the Island. Although casualties from these bombardments were usually light, the stress, fear and anxiety that resulted, made it tough to do our duty. The constant crashing of shells and explosions in or near our positions had a debilitating effect on our mind and senses.

The stepped-up volume of enemy artillery and gunboat bombardments seemed to be signaling a land attack that was going to be coming soon. This would be our first experience with a hostile enemy, who was trying to kill us.

Chapter 14

Our nights were now very much the same. We would see the bright flashes dancing above the horizon and hear the sound of the distant booms. Breaking the dark stillness, awaiting the approaching unknown were the crashing impacts and explosions landing on the Island.

We had visited Fort Wagner several times while performing duties around Charleston Harbor. We knew that the sounds of exploding shells were coming mostly from that direction. Taking Fort Wagner was critical to Union forces due to its strategic location on Morris Island, guarding the Harbor. If Confederate guns could be captured or silenced, the harbor was open to Union attack from the sea.

This morning would be very different from our normal routine. It had rained during the night and it was hot and muggy and the air was very still. Before the sun came up, we were awakened and told to get ready for possible action.

"Be prepared to move out quickly," said Lieutenant Hill. "Make sure you have everything. Check your musket, ammunition and water and take rations for two days."

An attack on Fort Wagner had been attempted earlier. It had failed but we knew another might be coming soon. We would be reinforcing other units in the area if there was to be another attack. It came as a surprise then that we were ordered to march in a direction away from Ft. Wagner, toward gunboat fire and the booms of cannons coming from our west.

"The Yanks have landed on the Island and they're moving this way. We have to stop them," said Lieutenant Hill.

The direction in which we were moving took us near a large marshy area. This would make our going slow because of knee deep mud, tall sharp grasses, crabs and nasty mosquitoes. We knew it would not be an easy march.

Most of us however, were ready for a fight. We had been in camp cleaning weapons, preparing our equipment and continuously drilling, so we felt we were ready to meet any enemy challenge. Also, we had grown very tired of being shot at without being able to see the enemy or fire back. It was now our turn to do some of the shooting.

We didn't have very long to wait. "Prepare to attack enemy positions," commanded Captain Peters. We could hear the cannon shells exploding closer and we suspected we weren't far from the enemy's forward lines.

A few moments later, from what seemed like an enemy squad or platoon, we started receiving musket fire on our left flank. We dropped immediately, seeking whatever cover we could find and prepared to return fire. I was quickly splattered in mud and water as I went down on my stomach. The sound of bullets buzzing above my head, grabbed my attention and I all but forgot my surroundings and discomfort.

Shortly after that, we heard a friendly unit to our right open fire. "Gentleman, get up. It's time. Load your weapons," Lieutenant Hill yelled. A few minutes later, he pointed in the direction of the enemy fire and yelled, "Charge."

With emotion and enthusiasm raging, we were quickly up and moving toward the enemy. Just a few minutes later however, we moved into a swampy area, that wasn't clearly visible in the darkness. We were soon taking labored steps as we slowly trudged through knee-deep mud and water.

As we forced our legs forward, moving very slowly, I kept thinking that I needed to keep my powder and musket dry and be ready to fire when ordered. We stopped about a hundred yards from where the firing was coming and prepared to return the fire. "Prepare to fire--ready, aim, fire," Lieutenant Hill commanded.

I aimed in the direction of the enemy and pulled the trigger. I saw the flash of my weapon but little else. I felt the jolt backward as I fired. I recovered and immediately began to reload. The air was filled quickly with the acrid sulfur smell of gunpowder.

As bullets continued to buzz overhead, I heard one hit its target about five yards to my right. The bullet struck Private Charles Reynolds, a soldier from a neighboring county who had joined the unit at about the same time as me. He was hit in the shoulder and was groaning loudly. As I got closer to him, I could see blood seeping through a tear in his coat, on his right shoulder.

"I'm hit, I'm hit," yelled Private Reynolds. I immediately kneeled down and tried to comfort him while calling for our unit surgeon. I could see from the expression on his face that he was in a lot of pain. I raised him up from the dampness of the ground and tried to make him as comfortable as possible.

"Lie still Charlie. You'll be okay," I said to him but not really knowing for sure.

"Am I going to die, Micah?"

"No Charlie, you're going to be okay. But you need to be still now. Help is coming." It appeared to be a shoulder wound and he didn't appear to be losing much blood so I was optimistic about his chances for recovery.

When help arrived, I wished him luck and then resumed moving in the direction of the enemy fire. I didn't realize it then but that was to be the last time I would ever see Charlie alive. I wish now that I had taken more time to say goodbye to him and something more meaningful than "Good luck Charlie."

I could see Daniel on my left about five yards to the front. When we reached the location where the enemy had been firing, it appeared that they had pulled back and quickly. Remnants of their brief occupation of the area were still on the ground. We couldn't see them now and they were not firing. We continued our slow movement forward.

After ten more minutes of labored movement through the marsh, Lieutenant Hill ordered us to stop. "Halt. Stop firing men. It looks like they've pulled back."

It was our first taste of fighting and it was over quickly. We knew we'd given it our best but it didn't seem like a victory. It didn't even seem like much of a battle.

We continued to hear musket fire several hundred yards to our right but there was no activity to our front. The enemy had attacked, got our attention but had then withdrawn. I wondered why they had done so without putting up much of a fight.

"Prepare to pull back men," Lieutenant Hill ordered. We began moving back into formation, trying as best we could in the water and mud and began our return back to camp. It was a small skirmish but it was our first real test of live fire with the enemy. We had just one casualty, sadly, Private Reynolds. The place where we had fought this day would now be embedded in our memories. It was called Grimball's Landing.

We later heard that we had fought with elements of the 54th Massachusetts Infantry. In a few days, their heroics would be etched in history leading a gallant charge, suffering severe losses in an unsuccessful attack on Fort Wagner.

A few weeks later, while in defensive positions in the sand hills surrounding the fort, we were attacked by a small Union force. We fought and held our positions courageously, suffering only minor casualties. We were commended for this effort. This turned out to be our last engagement on the Island.

In the weeks that followed, companies in our regiment continued to pull duty in and around Fort Wagner. The fort and the Island were soon abandoned and then occupied by Union forces.

Chapter 15

The Federals took control of Morris Island in September, 1863. We remained as part of harbor defenses in the Charleston area until April of the following year. Although Morris Island was abandoned and Fort Wagner reduced to rubble, both Fort Sumter and Charleston would remain under Confederate control until 1865 when General William Tecumseh Sherman marched his army into South Carolina.

In May of 1864, General Sherman was moving his army from Chattanooga toward Atlanta. If he was going there, we were too.

Our regiment's previous activity had been limited. Duty included several minor skirmishes and the preparation of defensive positions in the Charleston area. We had exposure to both naval and artillery gunfire in and around Morris Island, so we were good at keeping our heads down. Facing Sherman's army however, would be vastly different. It would be army against army, each maneuvering for advantage and trying to destroy the other.

Atlanta was a significant railroad, manufacturing and supply center in the South and a major prize for Sherman if he could take it. Just the psychological impact of the loss of Atlanta to the Confederacy would be catastrophic and certainly speed up its collapse. President Lincoln knew this and General Sherman did too. Lincoln needed a big victory to improve morale in the North and win his upcoming election. Atlanta was critical to the South. We knew it had to be defended.

The terrain in Northeast Georgia includes mountains, rolling hills, heavily forested areas and rivers which would test our regiment in ways it hadn't been before. It would also introduce us to large unit maneuvers, artillery barrages, trench warfare, sniper fire, hand-to-hand combat and cavalry charges that could come at any time to our front, flanks or even rear areas.

General Joseph E. Johnston's mission as given by Confederate President Jefferson Davis was to protect and defend Georgia by attacking and defeating the enemy. But Johnston would fight a defensive war by preventing the army from being outflanked and being careful not to expose his forces to a crushing defeat. Johnston didn't believe that he had the resources or strength to pursue an offensive campaign.

In June, our regiment moved toward Kennesaw Mountain, approximately, 20-miles north of Atlanta. Kennesaw is a Cherokee Indian name, "Gah-nee-saw" meaning cemetery or burial ground. The mountain is approximately eighteen hundred feet above sea level. It was steep in some areas, rocky with large boulders and heavily forested, providing good defensive positions for whoever held the ground. Both armies would meet there and we were moving quickly into position. For the next few days we would be preparing obstacles and constructing entrenchments to meet the enemy.

Sherman's army was larger than ours, almost twice the size. They were better equipped, better supplied and better fed. Their army was well-trained, experienced and gaining confidence as were most Union forces, especially since their victories at Vicksburg and Gettysburg, in July of '63. We were still confident however, that we could whip them with good leadership and under the right conditions.

On the morning of June 27th, the sky was overcast with a light drizzle. It had been that way for several days. The roads were muddy and puddles everywhere. We'd been preparing positions for several days and felt we were ready.

"The enemy's getting closer men. Hurry up and finish what you're doing. After the artillery bombardment, their attack will soon follow. Get yourselves ready. Make sure you're dug in deep and have good cover. We don't have much time now," Lieutenant Hill said. "And, for God's sake men, keep your heads down."

"We're ready sir," I replied. "Let them come. We're ready for a fight."

He gave me a quick glance and a stiff smile and then walked off toward the others. "Make sure your weapons and powder are dry and clean," he commanded. "You're going to need them today, that's for certain. We don't want any misfires."

Our position was next to Burnt Hickory Road running next to a large hill, a spur from Little Kennesaw Mountain. There were skirmishers in positions to our front manned by the 63rd Georgia Infantry. The enemy would have a tough time getting close to us, I thought. It would be slow going for them through a wet, almost swampy area and then dense thickets, all the time moving up a gradually rising hill.

In what seemed like only minutes since Lieutenant Hill had given us the warning, an artillery barrage of about fifty cannons opened up on us. Their roar was awesome and thunderous with the sound seeming to echo off the side of the mountain. I had never heard anything like this before. Not even the sounds of naval bombardments directed at Fort Wagner could compare to this. I was scared. The continuing volleys and booms threw whistling shells overhead, crashing into trees and impacting on the ground around us. Tree limbs were cracking and trees were toppling. The noise was deafening. Mud, rocks and debris were flying everywhere. My beard, unshaven for several days was splattered with mud. We kept our heads down and waited.

When the cannon fire had begun, I grabbed my weapon to keep it close. "Daniel, are you alright?" I yelled.

Daniel was about ten yards away from me on my right.

He gave me a quick look and a nod and said, "Keep your head down buddy and your eyes to the front. They'll be coming soon."

The artillery fire lasted less than a half-hour but it seemed much longer than that. We hunkered down in our rifle pits and trenches, prepared for whatever might be coming next. Our positions were at the edge of a tree line with the ground sloping down slowly in front of us. I looked out to our front and could see for only a few hundred yards. The enemy wouldn't be visible, I thought, until they came charging toward us.

When the cannon barrage ended, the damage was visible all around us. Trees and large limbs were down in every direction I looked. Breathing was tough. It seemed like I was inhaling mostly dust and smoke. It took several minutes before I was breathing normally again. I couldn't see anything to my front except a large, gray, slow moving cloud of smoke. In the distance we could hear yelling and shouting, the beating of drums and commands being given but we couldn't see detail through the thick haze.

Moments later, the smoke started to clear. We could see movement in the distance. At first it appeared as a hazy blue blob but then we began to see individual soldiers, in their blue uniforms, marching in formation and coming toward us.

They were getting closer now. I could hear the steady beat of their drums. On some other occasion, it might've seemed like a parade--the troops in blue, marching closely together, in a tight line with their colors flying. I even had a lazy thought for a moment that it might be fun to watch them, were it not for the deadly turmoil and barbarity that was soon to come.

We watched in awe but I knew that soon hundreds of us would be dead. It was an eerie feeling; a repugnant thought. My heart was pounding and my stomach knotting. My breathing quickened. I was torn between two emotions--should I prepare to fight or prepare for flight. I was hoping it wouldn't be the latter. I knew though that I had to stand and fight with my regiment. I would not be running, I said to myself. My brother, my friends and our lives were at stake here. Yes, I would make a stand with them today.

We waited as the enemy continued their movement forward. Our supporting artillery on the hills above was firing into their lines as they marched toward us. They fired at the blue masses with shot and canister, smashing holes into their lines. Our attackers moved into a double-quick step as they came closer. I heard yelling and firing out to our front where the 63rd Georgia was manning their rifle pits. There was evident confusion. I saw troops in gray running to the rear. I saw panic in their faces. I didn't know what was happening.

When Union troops were in full view, about a hundred yards to our front, we opened with massive musket fire. The initial volley from our weapons slowed and dropped many of those coming at us. Holes widened within their lines. Others rushed in to try and fill them.

We reloaded and fired our weapons again and again at will. I was tiring but I couldn't stop. Survival now depended on my ability to reload and fire accurately. My breathing was quick and heavy. I was perspiring uncontrollably. I knew that the next few minutes would determine if I would live or die.

"Keep firing men, keep firing. For God's sake men, keep firing!" Lieutenant Hill commanded.

The noise was deafening and the chaos was enveloping us. I had no time to think, only to fight. We continued to fire at the enemy for what seemed an eternity to me but was probably twenty minutes. The volume of our fire was continuous and heavy. The flashes and loud pops from our weapons must have been horrifying to those approaching our wall of lead. The air was heavy again with smoke and dust. It was getting harder to see and breathe. My arms and legs were aching from the repetitious loading and firing but I couldn't stop. I mustn't stop.

As the enemy got closer, their ranks were thinning. Many had fallen to the ground from their wounds or were struggling to find a place of temporary safety on a battlefield that was filled with death and destruction. Still, they kept coming forward and we continued firing. Some of our comrades had fallen from enemy fire but we remained determined to fight and stay in our positions.

When the remaining attackers were about fifty yards in front of us, they began to run fiercely toward us, screaming and hollering with an ungodly yell that echoed through the woods. We could see their faces clearly now. They had the look of kill in their eyes; like predatory animals attacking their prey.

Several of the enemy reached our positions as we continued firing. Many of my buddies were engaged in hand-to-hand fighting. As I reloaded, I looked quickly to my right and saw Daniel yank an enemy soldier down toward him. I then saw Jeb who was next to him bayonet another who was trying to enter their trench.

I finished reloading and quickly stole another glance over at Daniel. From the corner of my eye, I saw a soldier coming toward him with his bayonet extended. "Daniel," I yelled and then instinctively fired a shot at the attacker. I saw the soldier fall helplessly to the ground in front of him. I reloaded quickly.

The violence continued. For only a moment, it seemed like everything was in slow motion—soldiers fighting, muskets flashing, bayonets thrusting. I could see our guys firing from the trenches and others fighting hand-to-hand with the enemy. The struggle seemed to go on for another ten minutes.

Suddenly, the attack ended. We heard yelling to our front and then the soldiers who had been attacking us began falling back. Some retreated to positions previously held by the 63rd Georgia. Others were trying to withdraw but were pinned down, seeking cover from our musket and cannon fire. They even had to dodge huge boulders being rolled down the rocky hill toward them. The situation remained this way until darkness.

We could still hear movement, voices and cries of anguish out to our front but they grew fainter as the night progressed. I drifted in and out of sleep, exhausted, with my musket cradled in my arms.

When I awoke the next morning, I was not prepared for what I would see. I saw enemy soldiers slumped over the obstacles we had built days earlier. I saw them lying in our pits and trenches. I saw others scattered around on the ground to our front. Everywhere I looked, there were corpses in blue with splashes of mud and dried blood covering their uniforms. Some of the dead were older soldiers but mostly they were young. Miraculously, we found some still alive, moving though moaning in pain. Most were not moving at all.

I had viewed a sight that morning that I hoped I would never see again. I prayed to God that I could soon forget it--arms and hands, legs and feet dangling or separated from what were once healthy bodies; limbs that had separated from both the living and the dead. Only twenty-four hours earlier, these were fathers, sons, uncles and brothers now reduced to these lifeless forms. I stared at pools of dried blood which had mixed with mud and dirt to form a bizarre reddish color. I thought again of the cries, the anguish and the horror of it all. It was sickening. My head was aching and my stomach knotted. I was nauseous and later began to vomit.

We had captured and killed many that day. Their losses exceeded ours by about four to one. We had sustained casualties in the regiment but our losses were light compared to those in blue. As I surveyed the area to my front again, the carnage was incomprehensible. I had just witnessed and participated in human butchery. No one should ever have to be part of something like that, I thought to myself. I was heartbroken by the misery and pain in front of me. I was emotionally exhausted.

We had fought hard and won a victory. I should be happy now just being alive but I was not. My heart ached with the pain of so much loss, regardless of uniform color.

Later that morning, a brief truce began. A white piece of cloth attached to a stick, was waved in front of us from the other side. A soldier shouted, "Can we come get our dead?"

"Yea, go ahead. We won't fire," Captain Peters replied. Then they began to come out slowly, cautiously, to collect their dead. We too, attended to our wounded and dead and those captured in the fighting.

That afternoon was spent preparing for another attack. We rebuilt and improved our obstacles, our damaged rifle pits and trenches and were re-supplied with ammunition and other provisions. We prepared for a follow-up attack but it never came. Sherman began moving his army further to the south continuing to look for ways to flank us. He would test us again on another field, on another day but not today.

Our regiment had survived its first major battle. We were victorious and the regiment had performed well. In a few hours however, we would be on the march again. Where would we find General Sherman's army or where would he find us? I knew this day was one that I wouldn't soon forget. Unfortunately, I sensed there would be more days just like it to follow.

Chapter 16

Several weeks later in the month of July, General George H. Thomas and the Army of the Cumberland were moving south toward Atlanta and would soon have to cross Peachtree Creek. This was an opportunity for us to attack while his army was in a vulnerable situation--crossing the creek.

On the morning of the 20th we began moving into position for an attack. We knew that the Federals would be preparing defensive positions right after their crossing and it would be critical to hit them early, while they were just beginning those preparations.

Unfortunately, it didn't happen as planned and the attack didn't start until around 4 p.m., that afternoon. A lack of coordination at the command level was later blamed for allowing the Federals extra time to prepare and be ready to defend.

Our regiment moved to the front anticipating an attack against the Federal positions. We made preparations, checking our weapons and ammunition and then forming into a line for the attack. I could see my brother Daniel clearly. He looked ready, his musket pointed forward and his eyes focused sharply to the front. I asked him, "Daniel, are you alright?"

He looked at me and gave me a quick nod of his head and said "Yes." I could see Jeb to his right. Directly in front of me was Lieutenant Hill. We were waiting for the word to move out.

Lieutenant Hill had been a lawyer before the war. He was from Chatham County and his home was in Savannah. He had a likeable personality and had a good relationship with the soldiers in our unit. He liked to tell stories about some of the cases he had taken as a young lawyer. He was very entertaining and fun to be around. He didn't have any of the stuffiness or formality that we sometimes saw from the other officers. He was also knowledgeable of current events. He seemed to know what was happening at all times and tried to keep us informed. It was the Lieutenant in fact, who told us that General John Bell Hood had replaced General Johnston as our new Army commander.

"From what I hear, Johnston was too cautious in battle. That's why Davis replaced him with Hood. Hood will be more aggressive. He was severely wounded earlier in the war. He knows how to fight. He will fight," Lieutenant Hill said.

Actually, most of us thought caution was a good thing because the Union Army was much bigger than ours and General Sherman seemed to be continually trying to flank us. Since the Lieutenant had used the term aggressive, I assumed he meant there would be less defensive and more offensive operations for our Army. One thing was for sure--things would be changing.

Lieutenant Hill gave us the order to move out at quickstep, a fast walk. As we neared the enemy positions, we went to double-quick which was twice as fast as quickstep, a fast trot. Shortly thereafter we were given the command "Charge" and we began to run toward the enemy. Our regiment hollered and yelled as we ran toward the enemy positions in front of us. We were determined to break through them.

A tremendous volume of fire was directed back at us. I saw the flashes of their cannon and heard bullets whistling as they flew over our heads and crashed into the ground all around us, kicking up dust and smoke. Still, we continued forward. We were determined to succeed. Our mission was to break through enemy lines and we all knew it.

When we were about a hundred yards in front of the enemy, they opened up on us with hideous canister fire--little iron balls' flying toward us at murderous speed with each loud belch of their cannons. I noticed several soldiers to my left and right go down. Private Wilson was one of them. I quickly ran over to him but I could see there was nothing that could be done for him. He had been struck in the head and neck by several of the tiny iron balls. His head and flesh had been gashed open. He was barely recognizable. I got up quickly and resumed my forward march.

I saw our regimental flag bearer collapse to his knees, then fall to the ground after being hit in the head by a bullet. Daniel raced up and grabbed our colors and continued racing forward. Our regiment continued toward the enemy. The smoke and dust made it hard for us to see and breathe.

To our front were several fallen trees that had been knocked over by the anger of the opposing cannon. They were about fifty yards in front of the enemy. I rushed forward and took a position behind one of the larger ones. It provided me some protection from enemy fire. Several other soldiers moved up beside me. We aimed, fired our muskets and then began to reload.

I looked over to my right and I could see Daniel and several others moving toward an enemy trench. I saw Daniel and Jeb jump in, fighting hand to hand with the enemy. Those of us in position behind the downed trees continued firing.

I saw several enemy soldiers retreating from the pit where Daniel had been. "Come on," I yelled to those who were near me and I pointed to our front. We raced forward to the enemy trench. I saw Daniel and Jeb. Daniel had his bayonet facing two soldiers in the pit. He was standing over them. They were sitting with their heads down in the bottom of the trench, arms extended in the air.

I saw Jeb. He was sitting on the ground, leaning with his back against the side of the pit. I saw blood on the side of his coat. I ran over to him. "Jeb, how badly are you hurt?"

"I'll be okay. I got grazed by a bullet below my arm pit. I'll be fine."

"The surgeon's coming. He was right behind us. I'll try to find him."

I looked at Daniel and asked, "Are you okay?

"Yeah," he replied, "I captured a couple of yanks."

I could still hear weapons firing to our right. It sounded like the fighting was continuing. I went back to find the surgeon for Jeb, keeping my head low as I moved toward the rear.

It wasn't long after that, when I heard Lieutenant Hill order us to pull back. I found the surgeon and took him back to where Jeb was waiting in the trench.

"The Yankees are preparing to counterattack. Let's get out of here," Lieutenant Hill yelled.

"Jeb's been hit Lieutenant. We'll move as quickly as we can. We need to get Jeb back to the rear," I said.

"We're moving back to provide support to units on our right in case of counterattack," the Lieutenant said. Our unit then moved quickly to the rear, in the direction of our previous positions.

We helped Jeb walk to the rear for treatment. The surgeon quickly examined and then bandaged Jeb's wounds. "He'll be fine, Micah. He's a tough guy. His wound isn't that deep. He'll heal quickly."

After assisting with Jeb, I quickly rejoined my comrades. We had reformed and moved back several hundred yards to our immediate right. Quickly looking around, it seemed like we had lost several men during the assault. I had accounted for Daniel and Jeb but I wasn't sure who or how many were missing.

Reaching the new position, we prepared for an expected counterattack. It never came. On this day, Union troops had held their ground and our side had taken the greater casualties in both wounded and dead.

As the days followed, we stayed in close proximity to Sherman's army. Would they attack today? If so, where? Would we attack? If so, then when and where? As the defense of Atlanta continued, the armies maneuvered and engaged one another over the next several weeks with neither army achieving that decisive final victory.

Chapter 17

"Get your gear ready. We're moving out. We've got new orders." It was late in the afternoon on July 21 and we were preparing for another attack on Union positions when Lieutenant Hill spoke those words. We looked at him with surprised and puzzled faces. "General McPherson is moving the Army of the Tennessee west, from Decatur toward Atlanta. We'll be moving with all possible speed to meet him."

Our route of movement would take us north of Atlanta and then south and east for an attack on McPherson's Army. We would be part of Lieutenant General Hardee's Corps.

As a result of the fighting that had taken place on the 20th and our preparations for a counterattack on the 21st, all of us were suffering from a lack of sleep, hunger and fatigue. To make matters worse, the weather was very hot and muggy. But it didn't matter. The march would have to be made even if it took us all night. McPherson had to be stopped.

General Hood had taken over command of the Army of Tennessee just prior to the battle at Peachtree Creek. Although he was once a handsome, well-built man, the war had changed him significantly. His left arm now dangled at his side from a shrapnel wound he received at Gettysburg in July of 1863. His right leg had been amputated just below the hip from a wound he received at Chickamauga, two months later.

Some said that Hood suffered significant pain from his injuries and was taking medication for them. Whether this affected his decision-making is a matter of conjecture. However, he differed greatly from Johnston in his approach to the

Army--he was aggressive and wouldn't hold back. Where Johnston had been cautious and always seemingly, in delaying actions, Hood was not afraid to act quickly and boldly. Some even thought his actions were impulsive. This sometimes caused trouble for the army because our attacks seemed to lack the necessary coordination at corps and division level required for success.

Our mission was to strike McPherson's army by surprise when unable to defend itself. Unfortunately, our road march was delayed due to poor road conditions, inadequate scouting and fatigue. The delay in getting into position allowed McPherson time to improve his defensive posture and to put his XVI Corps in perfect position to defend against an attack.

On the morning of July 22nd, we began our assault. To attack McPherson, we had to go through thick underbrush, which was painful to exposed arms and legs and slowed our movement. As we emerged from the woods, the Federals were directly to our front. Horrendous volleys of musket fire and devastating canister from Union cannon welcomed us to the battlefield.

Several attempts to overrun Federal positions were only partially successful. On the second attempt, we reached the enemy's lines and fierce hand-to-hand combat ensued. I remember only a small part of that encounter. I had aimed and fired at an enemy soldier about fifty yards to my front. I saw him fall as the bullet struck him. Moments later, an enemy soldier came at me from the side and was about to impale me with his bayonet when Daniel jumped him at the last moment. But I don't remember much after that. I had paused for a moment watching Daniel wrestle the combatant to my left and then someone clubbed me in the head from the right. I was unconscious for several hours after that.

"Are you okay?"

"What happened? Where am I? Who are you?" I said with blurry eyes to someone above me.

"I'm the regimental surgeon. You were brought here by your brother. It appears that you took a blow to the head, judging by the size of the knot up there. You've lost some blood, too. You've been unconscious for about four hours. You're in a field hospital wagon now and you should feel better in a few hours. Just try to remain still and get some rest."

"How did we do today?"

He looked around and then continued, "Based on what I heard earlier, each of our attempts succeeded in reaching Union positions. We captured cannon and prisoners but were turned back by Federal counterattacks. We took heavy losses-- many were killed and wounded. I haven't seen this much carnage in a long time. It's been a very rough day."

"How're you feeling Micah?" Daniel asked, coming to see me about an hour later.

"I'm okay but I have a bad headache. I hear we didn't do so well today. What did you see?"

"We hit them several times but took a lot of casualties. Jimmy Patterson was shot in the right leg, just above the knee and was moved to the rear. I haven't seen him yet." He paused, looked at the ground and then up at me and said, "Johnny Williams was killed by enemy cannon fire."

Johnny was from a nearby farm which I visited many times as a kid. He had traveled with Daniel and me to join the 54th early in 1862. I was saddened by this news as we had grown up together and had spent many days playing in the woods and fishing on the Altamaha. "Johnny was a good soldier and friend to me. I'll miss him very much."

"Me too," said Daniel.

I thought of Johnny's parents and the grief they would be feeling from this news. It's bad enough when a family loses a son but in this case, he was their only son. Johnny also had three sisters back home.

I heard later that General James B. McPherson, who had commanded the army against us, had been shot and killed by a sniper as he rode on his horse near the front lines. Soldiers of all ranks and ages had died on this day but General McPherson was the second highest ranking union officer to be killed during this war. He was almost thirty-six.

"Another day and many more good souls on both sides have been killed and maimed today Daniel and for what? There have been so many lives thrown away, in this hell. It just goes on and on and on. Why would a good and merciful God let this butchery go on, Daniel? Why doesn't he just end it? Why does it seem he has turned his eyes away from us? Doesn't he care? When will this misery end?"

"I don't know Micah. I don't think anyone has the answer to that. Maybe he just doesn't approve of war and has turned his back on all of this. We may not have much time left either. I don't know. But let's not talk about this anymore today."

The rest of July and August was surprisingly quiet. There were fewer of us now, though we hoped replacements would be coming soon. The war was dragging on and we had learned the routine well: maintain our weapons and equipment daily, squeezing in time for meals and rest while waiting for the inevitable; march to battle; prepare for an attack or to be attacked; find, fight and kill enemy soldiers; be prepared for a counterattack while attending to the dead, wounded and captured and all of this while dealing with the extremes of weather. Our ranks, our friends, our fellow soldiers grew smaller in number every day, as we repeated this horrible routine.

Chapter 18

We remained vigilant in August and continued to improve our positions. As always, we were ready to move on a moment's notice. Staying prepared for all possibilities was challenging but critical to our unit and personal survival.

One evening, while sitting around in camp we began to hear cannon fire coming from the direction of Atlanta. We could see bright flashes in the distance and the rumbling booms that followed. General Sherman's artillery was firing into the city. Confederate artillery was returning his fire. This bombardment went on for several days with significant destruction of buildings and property throughout Atlanta and the loss of life, both military and civilian. Those who were unable to evacuate the city were forced to seek shelter in cellars or secure buildings until the cannonades subsided.

We learned of the horror occurring in Atlanta from fleeing refugees making their escape from the city. "Our homes, our lives are being destroyed," a woman passing on the road in front of us said as she looked toward us in desperation. She wore an old cotton dress that was torn and dusty and was accompanied by two young girls, who I assumed were her daughters looking both tired and frightened. They were walking beside an old cart being pulled by a mule which appeared to be carrying their salvaged belongings.

"Can't you do anything? Won't you try and stop them? Will you help us? People are dying back there," she said, pointing and looking back at Atlanta. We felt helpless, listening to her and ignoring her pleas. I turned my face away from the sadness in her eyes. They must be the lucky ones, I thought, being able to escape the city between artillery exchanges. Not everyone was so fortunate.

It was frustrating for us to look at her and hear her pleading, knowing there was little we or anyone could do now to avert the disaster that was occurring in Atlanta or to slow the inevitable march of Sherman. I looked back at her one last time and with teary eyes, just shook my head slowly.

After a few days and an apparent lull in the fighting, we figured that Sherman had withdrawn his Army away from Atlanta since we no longer heard the cannonades or felt the pressure of enemy pursuit. This turned out to be just partly true. Sherman knew that he couldn't capture Atlanta without destroying the railroads that were supplying the city from the south. The Atlanta and West Point Railroad led southwest and the Macon and Western Railroad led southeast, toward Macon. Sherman decided to destroy them.

Earlier Union cavalry raids had not shut down the railroads. Tracks, at different locations, would be torn up one day but then confederate soldiers or local sympathizers would quickly repair them the next. So, Sherman decided to send his infantry to complete the job. If these railroads were destroyed, he reasoned, Hood would have to evacuate the city. There wouldn't be any open lines for re-supply of his army.

During the last week of August, the federals began their task of destroying the rail lines heading south. Rails were dug up, heated, twisted and discarded making their repair almost impossible. When Hood realized what was happening, he sent General Hardee and two Corps to Jonesborough to try to interrupt these operations.

We traveled by train all night and by mid-afternoon of the next day we were set to attack federal positions. We knew the fate of Atlanta was at stake. What we didn't know then was that most of Sherman's army would be there also and we would be facing almost impossible odds.

We attacked two federal corps to our front but were unable to alter the tactical situation. As a result, on the morning of September 1st, the positions of the opposing forces had barely changed. Hood, hearing the day's results and fearing an attack on Atlanta decided to pull one Corps away from Hardee and back to the city. We were now facing a much larger force on the battlefield that included Sherman's IV and XIV Corps.

The federals attacked us on our right flank and even though we fought bravely and gallantly, our positions were overrun. We avoided a total disaster by some maneuvering and heroic actions to reinforce the holes in our lines that the Federals had achieved. We were forced to pull back after taking large numbers of casualties and many taken as prisoners.

When night arrived, we retreated several miles down the road to a place called Lovejoy Station. There, we dug-in and prepared for another assault by Union forces. However, learning that Hood had abandoned Atlanta, Sherman decided to disengage from the battle and return to Atlanta instead.

Later that evening, when I had time to reflect on the actions of the day, I considered for a moment some of our losses. Private Terrell Anderson, a new father, had been killed by a cannon shell that had burst overhead. Captain William Peters, our company commander, had been shot and killed while directing our withdrawal from the battlefield. Private Wayne Johnson had been captured by the enemy.

I listened in as Lieutenant Hill described how it happened. "I saw Private Johnson fall but I didn't think he was hurt that badly at first. It looked like he had a wound in his leg and was having some trouble getting up. I wasn't that close to him, so I couldn't respond to his cries for help. I then saw four enemy soldiers rush over and then hurriedly drag him away. He was hollering all the while but at least he was still alive. I wish I could've done more but I wasn't able to." Hill looked away then and said tearfully to those of us standing nearby, "I hope he'll be okay. He was a good soldier."

This was the last action of the Atlanta campaign and it meant that Atlanta had fallen. On September 1-2, General Hood evacuated the city. Without the ability to supply Atlanta by rail, Hood had concluded that the city could not be held. As the remainder of Hood's units withdrew from Atlanta, buildings and supplies were burned by his men. Anything that could be of use to the Federals, was ordered destroyed by Hood.

"Can you believe that we're seeing this?" Daniel asked as we marched down the road.

"I see it Daniel but I can't believe it. Who would've ever thought this could happen? I never expected the war to come this far south. Atlanta captured and destroyed, it's crazy."

The bright glow of fires lit up the horizon and loud explosions could be heard throughout the night. Dark smoke rising from the ashes of Atlanta could be seen for miles and miles as we marched the next day. There was great sadness all around as most of us sensed this was the beginning of the end for our army, the Confederacy and a way of life.

Chapter 19

At the end of November General Hood, not overly-cautious and known to be aggressive, was pushing northward hoping to find and destroy the Army of Ohio, commanded by Major General John M. Schofield. During the night of November 29th, Schofield's army had passed by Hood undetected at Spring Hill and now an agitated Hood was trying to catch up to him. Hood's objective was to destroy Schofield's army before it could join Union forces under General Thomas gathering in Nashville.

Hood moved north toward Franklin, Tennessee, on November 21st. Our regiment, now part of Brigadier General James A. Smith's Brigade, was assigned to detached duty and left behind in the area of Florence, Alabama on the Tennessee River. It was our mission to guard the supply train while the army chased Schofield.

The supply train contained the provisions for the army including rations, ammunition and pontoons for crossing rivers and all other necessary essentials required by a mobile army. Being an attractive target, we would be on guard against attacks by enemy skirmishers, cavalry and even bands of brigands or deserters.

Temperatures were now steadily dropping. During the summer months, we despised the itchy wool blouses which were part of our uniform but they were understandingly more welcome during the colder and wetter winter months. Most of our uniforms were torn and tattered. Many soldiers were without boots or if they had them, they were in poor shape. Muddy roads added to our misery and made marches difficult. Some of us still had blankets but they were badly worn and in short supply. There were opportunistic times however, when the spoils of battle provided items of clothing and equipment from our better outfitted northern adversaries.

Fires were lit every night in camp to keep us warm and dry, using any available wood or other flammable substance we could find. Sometimes when the breeze was light, it would be so smoky from our fires that it was hard to see the layout of the campsite.

If we were fortunate, there would be wooded areas nearby providing an ample supply of firewood. At other times fence rails from farms, wood from abandoned barns and farmhouses or the remnants of torn up railroad ties would be our source to keep the fires burning. As we marched along dirt roads, eyes were always open for new sources of firewood.

"Micah, you and Daniel go find some wood. It's your turn to do the scavenging," said Sergeant Walker. "I want to stay warm tonight so find lots of dry wood. Don't come back here till you do."

"Daniel, I saw an old wagon near that deserted farm we passed about a mile back. That wood should still be good. There were also some downed tree limbs by a nearby stream. This shouldn't take us too long."

"I saw it too. Let's hope it isn't rotten or soaked from the rains. I don't want this duty to take too long tonight."

Guarding the wagon train wasn't easy. Although we had sufficient soldiers to defend against a limited attack, the wagons were sometimes strung out for several miles along the road making it even more difficult. This happened when we stopped for the night in an area without a large clearing for our campsite.

Although the war had reduced the size of our wagon train significantly, we still had almost four hundred wagons to guard. Also, the caring and feeding of the horses and mules required time and patience.

Normally, there would be a wagon park and the necessary individuals to provide for the feeding and caring of the animals and maintenance of the wagons. Sometimes we would be detailed to assist in the effort. Depending on our location and the time of year this duty could be easy or downright difficult.

"Go tend to the horses and mules my lads," Sergeant Walker commanded to those soldiers whose turn it was to do the duty. It was an undesirable but necessary duty.

I actually liked working with the animals because it reminded me of my days back on the farm. But the mules, they could be very stubborn at times. Mules are strong and can do with less food than a horse so they are very useful to an army. The problem is they don't do anything they don't want to do. I think that stubbornness was from just being careful not to hurt themselves or being afraid of something. As a soldier, I understood that. I remember one time when I was trying to cross a small stream and something spooked the mule I was leading. I tried several times to cross but the mule wouldn't budge. I eventually had to move upstream a ways to get my stack of wood back to camp. Maybe he heard a snake moving through the grass and that scared him. I never knew the real answer to that.

The animals had to be cleaned, fed and provided with fresh water and since feed was sometimes in short supply, foraging for food for the animals was also necessary. Many of the animals were underfed and undernourished. Their appearance was almost sickly at times. If we were near a large grassy field in the summer, the animals could feed themselves. In the winter though, food was scarce and more effort was required to find what they needed. Sometimes a nearby farm and a friendly farmer could provide the necessary resources. Mostly, our fellow southerners were sympathetic and obliging. Occasionally they weren't. Not only did we have to dodge bullets from the Yanks but sometimes an unfriendly farmer as well.

"What are you boys looking for?" an irritated farmer in Alabama said to us as we approached his barn one late afternoon. Sergeant Walker had sent us on a foraging mission for the animals in camp. We were running short on food and other items necessary for them.

"We need hay and salt for our horses and mules. Can you help us sir?" I asked.

"Sorry boys. I can't. We had a dry planting season and I have to rely on what we have left to get us through the winter. You boys are going to have to go look elsewhere," he said, lifting his shotgun slowly in our direction.

"But our army needs it. We can't win this war if we can't care for our animals," I pleaded.

"Well, it seems to me you've been getting your butts kicked lately anyway and I don't have anything extra to give you. So, get moving."

"Okay mister. We get your point. No need to get angry at us. We're leaving now," I said, as we slowly turned and walked away. We knew then, that this duty could sometimes be more difficult and dangerous than we might like it to be.

The animals required clean and fresh water also. If we were located near a fresh running brook or stream, that made our task easier. At other times, we had to look for water. Another chore was heating the chilled or frozen water in winter. We had to do that so the animals could drink it. Taking care of our animals wasn't easy but it was essential for the movement of the army. Being farm boys, Daniel and I realized that necessity and we usually didn't complain.

Over time though, we started noticing other changes. "I don't remember our animals back home looking like this," Daniel said to me one day as we were caring for them. "These animals need an end to this war too, so they can have a decent meal."

"Seems like we're losing more horses and mules each week--it's probably from the shortage of food or maybe just plain old exhaustion. If we can't take care of them, how're they going to take care of us?" I asked.

"We've been moving so fast, for so long they're beginning to look like us--tired, exhausted, underfed and beat," Daniel said. "I wonder how we're going to be able to fight the next time we meet the enemy. Look at us. We no longer even look like an army. We look like a disorganized group of sickly, disabled stragglers walking down the road together."

"I'll tell you the truth Daniel, I can't wait to get home and back to our quiet life as farmers. I miss it. I miss the farm, the animals and even the work. I love waking up early in the morning and seeing the sunrise. I love hearing the rooster's crow. I miss mom's breakfast. I want that life again. I want it real bad."

"I hope Mother and Father have been able to keep up with the farm. They haven't said anything in their letters to us, have they Micah? Mother probably wouldn't say if there were problems back home."

On November 30th, Schofield reached Franklin. He immediately occupied and improved the defensive positions that still remained from the previous battle there, in 1863.

Hood arrived later that afternoon and launched frontal assaults on strong Union positions. The confederates took huge losses including six generals that were killed or received mortal wounds. The Union held their positions and we were forced to withdraw. The battle of Franklin almost destroyed Hood's army, crippling it and its capabilities for the remainder of the war.

When the news reached the wagon trains, it was devastating. "The army took a terrible beating yesterday at Franklin. We took thousands of casualties and don't have much to show for it. The army is regrouping now and moving towards

Nashville. A big fight is coming there too, that's for sure. We're going also. Start packing and get ready to move out," Lieutenant Hill said to us.

We looked at each other with sorrow and fear. We knew that many of the soldiers killed at Franklin were men we had known, lived and fought with in the previous year. Many of them were from other regiments we had met and become friends with in camp. We were also feeling a sense of danger and futility for the days and months that still lay ahead of us.

"This army can't last much longer, Daniel. We're losing too many men. We can't overcome this. Just look around, everyone here is exhausted, weary or sick. Our clothing and equipment hardly protect us from the weather anymore. We're not getting any replacements. Certainly not fast enough. This can't go on much longer. We're near the end."

"You're right, Micah. But it will go on. It'll go on until there are none of us left to fight this war."

Chapter 20

After the disaster at Franklin, with the loss of about 6,000 men and six Confederate General Officers, Hood moved his Army north again looking to confront General Thomas at Nashville. Our brigade received orders to move north and join the army near Nashville.

We arrived on December 6th but a short time later, were sent east to join Major General Nathan Forrest's units near Murfreesboro. We spent the next several days tearing up the Nashville & Chattanooga Railroad between Nashville and Murfreesboro.

After delaying for about two weeks, General Thomas attacked Hood's forces just south of Nashville on December 15th. Much to the displeasure of the Union high command, a delay had resulted from both Thomas' careful planning of the attack and a snow and ice storm and sub-freezing temperatures in the days prior. Over the two day battle, our outnumbered Confederate army took another devastating defeat at the hands of Union forces.

When the news arrived from the battle at Nashville, we were ordered toward Pulaski, about fifty miles to the southwest. There, we would be in a defensive role, providing rear-guard protection for the army as it retreated from Nashville.

We immediately departed on a forced march. As our army moved south, we knew that the enemy would be following close behind in hot pursuit.

Our regiment, which originally comprised ten companies, was now down to about 168-men, barely enough for two companies. Although we occasionally saw replacements, they had slowed to a trickle now as other units had a higher priority.

The weather was wet and cold; the roads were muddy and difficult. It was a tough march as we continued to suffer from severely worn clothing and boots. We could barely keep together as we marched.

"Damn it, I hate this mud," Daniel said in an elevating voice, as I watched him struggle with each step forward.

"It reminds me of the swamps near Charleston," I said. "At least nobody is shooting at us now."

"Yeah, but they will be soon enough buddy. The Yanks aren't going to let us get away this time. They'll keep coming and coming until they catch and kill us all."

"That's why we're heading to Pulaski. We've got to protect what's left of the army. We have to help our brothers get home alive, Daniel. We've got to do it. They'd do it for us; you know they would."

We moved behind the retreating columns near Columbia. Our depleted units had been combined with Colonel Palmer's Brigade to increase the overall strength. Palmer was now our commander.

As we continued the march south, Union cavalry were pressing us at every turn. They would get close, feign an attack, and then withdraw. Our commander decided to make a stand. We moved into a line formation on the edge of the woods and waited for the next contact by Union cavalry. We didn't have long to wait.

"I can hear them. They're coming again boys. "Get ready to fight," Lieutenant Hill hollered.

As the mounted troops came around the bend, across from where we were hiding in the tree line, they attacked our skirmishers again. The skirmishers fell back toward us as they had before. This time, we didn't retreat.

"Fire your damn weapons boys. Give them hell now. Make sure they remember who we are," Lieutenant Hill shouted. We let go with a murderous volley on the attacking cavalry. I watched as horses and mounted soldiers dropped from the devastating fire we'd unleashed on them. We fired several more volleys with similar results.

Then Lieutenant Hill yelled, "Charge." Our line began rushing toward the attackers. The air around us quickly filled with dark smoke but we could still see the enemy to our front. We rushed forward. With our unexpected charge we captured several Union soldiers, their horses and one artillery piece, a 12-pounder, Napoleon. We continued pushing them back until we could no longer see them. Those remaining retreated out of view.

Our charge, just north of Pulaski, had reduced the immediate enemy threat and enabled us to continue moving south and cross the Tennessee River at Florence. It was the end of the Franklin-Nashville campaign, which had been a disaster for the Confederate army. The Army of Tennessee would no longer be a viable fighting force in the war.

The continuing losses were too much for the army to sustain. It was clear now that we were beaten. As the end of 1864 approached, most of us believed the war would soon be over. I believe that all of us were now quietly hoping if not praying, that would be the case.

Chapter 21

As the remnants of Hood's army retreated south, what had once been a substantial fighting force of over 39,000 men, before the Battle of Franklin, was now less than 10,000. The army was broken and virtually destroyed by the battles at Franklin and Nashville.

As Hood's army retreated from Nashville, General Sherman and the Union forces were advancing toward Savannah. It was captured just before Christmas, 1864. The Army of Tennessee continued on toward Tupelo, Mississippi where General Hood resigned his command.

Sherman began his march toward the Carolinas in February, 1865. He had a force of over 60,000 men. General Joseph E. Johnston, who was again the commander of The Army of Tennessee, had fewer than 10,000.

A number of smaller battles took place in the months of February and March. On March 19th, our army was located near Bentonville, North Carolina. The army had grown to about 21,000 with the addition of troops from General Braxton Bragg, who had abandoned Wilmington.

At Bentonville, on March 19th, Union Major General Henry W. Slocum and his Army of Georgia encountered entrenched Confederate troops. As skirmishing began, we prepared for what would be our final assault of the war.

"We're near the end, Daniel. I can feel it. We'll make a noble charge today but this is the end. Take care of yourself. Don't expose yourself foolishly. Mother wants us both to come home, alive."

"I will Micah. You do the same. I think you're right. This may be the end. We can't go on much longer. We're barely an army now. Keep your head down and protect yourself. Don't do anything stupid. You've been a good little brother," he said with a grin.

I smiled and then began to prepare my musket and equipment for the attack. I prayed that we'd both be alive at the end of the day. I knew the odds were against it.

Late that afternoon, our army attacked the XIV Corps under Brevet Major General Jefferson C. Davis. The attacks were successful. We drove the Union troops almost a mile from their original positions. We attacked again and again but were unable to overrun them. Finally, counterattacks and desperate fighting by Union forces, including newly arrived troops from the XX Corps, stopped our attack.

On the 20th, fighting was sporadic as the two armies consolidated their positions and prepared for further battle. Fighting continued on the 21st with a Union attack into the Confederate flank and rear areas. Fierce fighting and counter-attacks stopped the union advance and later that night, General Johnston and our army retreated across the bridge at Bentonville, toward Raleigh.

On April 9th, we received word that General Lee had surrendered the Army of Northern Virginia at Appomattox Court House in Virginia. The unexpected news shocked us. "What does that mean? Are we still at war Lieutenant?" I asked Hill.

"It means the end is getting much closer, Micah. If Lee has surrendered, I don't think we'll last much longer either. The Confederacy is collapsing. The war is almost over."

On April 18th, three days after the death of President Lincoln, General Johnston met with General Sherman to sign an armistice. After military and political terms for surrender were rejected by the cabinet in Washington, Jefferson Davis advised Johnston to disband the infantry and escape with his mounted troops. Johnston disobeyed knowing the situation was hopeless and agreed to a military surrender to Sherman. With the remnants of Johnston's army in Greensboro and Sherman's army in Raleigh, the surrender was accepted at the Bennett Place, just west of Durham, on April 26th.

The armistice included the surrender of all confederate forces, approximately 89,000 men in Alabama, the Carolina's, Georgia, Florida and Tennessee. It was the largest surrender of military forces during the war. With the surrender of smaller forces in Alabama and the Trans-Mississippi in New Orleans, within a month, the Confederate Army and the Confederacy were finished.

Chapter 22

At Guilford County Court House, Greensboro, North Carolina we surrendered our weapons, received our paroles and were given final pay. It wasn't much--less than two dollars and in Mexican currency.

About 16,000 confederates were paroled. Many more had deserted in the days and weeks prior when it appeared the war was nearly over. It was an emotional moment for us--to have been through so much and now it was ending. There would be no more marching, no more fighting, no more Confederacy. It was hard to believe. We were truly going home at last. It was a strange moment of both despair and happiness.

When General Lee surrendered at Appomattox, there was sadness as to the impending end of the Confederacy. Following the surrender at Durham, there was relief--relief that the fighting was finally over. With great destruction throughout the South, we didn't know what to expect when we returned home but we were relieved just the same and happy to be going.

"We're going home Daniel. I didn't think this day would ever come or if we would live to see it, but we have."

"It's odd. I can't believe it's over. Why is it over? After so much fighting and dying, for so long and now, suddenly, for it to end like this, just doesn't seem real to me yet," said Daniel.

"But it is and we'll soon be home with mother and father. I'm looking forward to seeing the farm again."

"Me too, Micah. Me too."

The Union troops treated us with respect and kindness, though it took several days to complete our transition. We were able to get fresh food, water and coffee for the first time in a long while. It was nice also to be able to sit down, eat and relax and not have to watch over our shoulders for enemy activity. It felt strange, that new sense of security and very odd.

I thought about how long it would take, perhaps weeks, months or even years to lose the constant fear of death we had been living with for the last several years. The anxiety of surprise attacks, cannon and sniper fire at any hour of the day or night, and from any direction, would be difficult to remove from our memories. I was having horrible dreams now. Would they go away with the war being over? I wondered.

We received our parole agreeing not to take up arms against the Union again. We were also given the right of passage for our route home. We looked forward to getting back, not knowing what we would find but still anxious to be going. Some talked about loved ones they longed to see, others about their farms and homes but most were just happy that the war was over and we could get back to what we assumed would be our normal lives. The war was over now. Daniel and I would have a peaceful journey home and then get back to our lives as ordinary farmers.

Chapter 23

We started for home in early May. The distance from Greensboro, North Carolina to our farm in Southern Georgia was approximately three hundred miles. We figured we could make it home in three weeks or less depending on the weather and road conditions. Since we were anxious to get home, it might take us less time if we could catch some rides along the way.

Our journey would take us through South Carolina and into Georgia passing through swamp and marshland areas. There were about eight who started the journey together. A few of us were from the same regiment but others were from other units that we met while waiting to receive our paroles. Most in the group would depart along the route or by the time we got close to Savannah.

"I can't wait to get home and see mother and father," I said to Daniel. "We've been gone for almost three years. Things have changed but hopefully, not too much. Mother hasn't mentioned anything in her letters but I know she usually keeps bad news to herself."

"I wonder how Aliyah is doing," Daniel said softly, like he was speaking to himself.

"What did you say? I thought that was in the past Daniel. Do you still have feelings for her?" I asked.

"I was just wondering how she's doing--how things are going on Aaron's farm. The war has touched our lives in many ways. I just wondered if she's okay."

"Mother hasn't mentioned Aliyah. She said that Pearl was doing fine and I assumed that she would have mentioned Aliyah if she wasn't okay. I hope father is alright. Every time I hear from mother she says he's doing fine but I'm not so sure. When Sherman's army was marching toward Savannah, they weren't too far from our farm. I just hope everything is okay back there."

"I'm sure things are, Micah. Mother would've said something in her letters if otherwise. Don't worry so much."

We left Greensboro heading south and others were making that same journey. There were groups of soldiers passing in both directions—some going north and others heading south but most were heading south. Some rode horses, some rode in wagons but most of those who we passed were walking just like us.

We'd been traveling south for three days and had walked all morning on the fourth day, when I heard Adam, a fellow traveler ask, "Hey guys. Do you want to take a break?" Adam had been with the 37th Georgia Infantry during the war and we met him just before we started for home. He was a small, quiet soldier but very personable and likable. "I see a stream up ahead. Maybe we should stop there for a while. We've been walking for quite a while and my dogs are aching."

"I bet they stink too. You'd better wash them off real good in that stream," said Daniel, jokingly.

"That sounds like a good idea Adam," I said. "I need to let my feet rest a while too." I'd been walking barefooted for the last few weeks and the soles on my feet looked like worn, badly weathered leather. I could only dream about what it would be like to have a new pair of shoes. I had spent almost one whole day thinking about shoes just before we got paroled. I imagined putting a slick shine on them too. Maybe when I get home I'll buy a pair, I thought to myself. I then paused, chuckled silently, thinking that I didn't even have enough money to buy a new pair of shoes.

The stream where we stopped was quiet and serene, almost pastoral. There were large oak trees bordering the small meandering stream with a pleasant breeze blowing through them. I could even hear birds chirping from up in the tops of the branches. I imagined one of those French artists setting up his canvas and painting this lovely scene. It would be a nice break from the hot dusty trail we'd been traveling.

"Boy that feels good," Daniel said as he stuck his feet in the cool water. "That water is nice; so very nice. I may have to stay here a few days or, maybe even a few weeks. Shucks, I may even build my farm right here."

"We should try to catch some fish while we're here," Adam said. "Sure would make for a nice supper."

"I doubt there are any fish in this stream that are stupid enough to let us catch them, especially once they get a smell of us. But if you see anything, maybe I'll try. I wouldn't mind some fresh fish for a change," Daniel replied.

We were stopped for about thirty minutes when four soldiers, on horseback, came up to stream where we were relaxing. They looked like they might have been cavalrymen; maybe from Forrest' unit, I thought. They were wearing confederate gray.

"How're you boys doing? Mind if we water our horses here?" one of them asked.

"Go ahead. Take care of your horses," Daniel said.

"The heat and dust are making us all very thirsty. We've been riding for several hours. My name is Cartwright," said the one doing the talking. He was tall, had a dark complexion, a closely cropped beard and seemed to be older than the others. He was wearing a uniform that was in better shape than what we had. He was also wearing a worn forage cap, typical of cavalry units. But there seemed to be something suspicious about him, I thought to myself.

"Where're you boys heading?" Cartwright asked.

"We're heading past Savannah to farming country just southwest of there," I said. "What about you?"

"We're heading to northern Florida. Our ranches are there and we need to get home. We haven't been back in quite a while. We were following and harassing Sherman's wagon trains. At least up until a few weeks ago. We caused Mr. Sherman a lot of headaches. We were always a pain in his backside."

"You were in the cavalry?" I asked.

"Yeah, we served with General Forrest. He was a good soldier. He kept us after those Yankees. It only took a few hundred of us to tie down thousands of Sherman's soldiers protecting the wagon trains. We shouldn't have quit. We could have won this thing. Now there's going to be a big price for the South to pay."

"Well, I'm glad it's over now. I just want to get home. We all have farms that need to be worked," I replied.

"Boys, we'd better be heading out," said Cartwright, as he looked slowly at each of his companions. The others just nodded. "You boys be safe."

"Thanks. You too," said Daniel.

"Oh, by the way, you boys have any money?" asked Cartwright, as he showed us a revolver in his right hand? "Why don't you boys just empty your pockets and give us what you've got."

"What are you doing Cartwright?" Daniel blurted out in anger. "We're soldiers just like you. We don't have much. Can't you see that? We were just paroled. We have very little of value on us."

"Well, just the same, turn your pockets inside out and then stick your hands up in the air. Boys, take a look and see if they have anything we want," he said, looking at his companions again. "They may have something we need. If you don't find money, a watch or something else, then take their blankets and canteens."

"Cartwright, we still have a ways to go and we need those things. You can't leave us on the road without them," I said.

"Shut up boy or you won't be needing anything but a hole in the ground," Cartwright said.

"They don't have much Cartwright," one of his companion's said. "Let's get out of here before someone comes along."

"Maybe we should just shoot one of them so the rest won't follow us," Cartwright said. He paused for a moment looking at us and then said, "Well, you boys had better forget that you saw us or the next time we won't be so nice to you."

The four of them then mounted their horses and road away heading south, in the direction of Florida. We hadn't started home with very much and now we had even less.

"We have no money, no canteens and no blankets," I said. "This journey has just gotten a lot tougher."

"Don't worry. We're going to make it. We've lasted too long and have gone through too much, to not make it," Daniel said. He then looked back toward Cartwright and the others as they rode away in the distance. "I hope I meet up with him again one day. He'll have a price to pay."

"This war has turned some good people bad and other's downright evil," Adam said. "I just want to get home and start my life over. I'm tired of all of this hatred and violence. I've seen enough ugliness to last me a lifetime. I just want to get home and back to farming."

Chapter 24

Our journey home was mostly uneventful after the meeting with Mr. Cartwright at the stream. Though we had to walk most of the way, we were able to catch an occasional ride on a wagon with a friendly farmer going our way. That made the journey a little easier on our feet. We were anxious to get home so we were happy with anything that made the trip take less time.

"How long you boys been gone?" asked the farmer, who had picked us up just south of Florence, South Carolina.

"It's been about three years, though it seems a hell of a lot longer than that. Luckily, we're coming home with our lives and limbs," said Daniel.

"A lot has happened since you boys were gone. The South is much, much different now. Nothing is the same. Plantations are in ruin. The slaves have left for the cities. Farms are smaller now and can barely provide a livelihood. Many were burned or destroyed by Sherman's soldiers. The markets where we use to take our harvest are either gone or are just starting to recover from the war. Our cities and towns have been destroyed or were badly damaged and citizens have deserted them. Survival has gotten much, much tougher for everyone. Marauders have ravaged what property Sherman's men didn't steal or destroy. No one is safe now and nobody can be trusted. You have to protect your property and watch everyone. You don't know who to believe. This war has released a terrible dark evil on our land."

I looked at Daniel. "We've got to get home, even if we have to travel day and night. We've got to get back to our folks and the farm. They probably need us now more than ever."

We came to a fork in the road where one way led to Charleston and the other to Savannah. "Well, this is it for me. I'll be leaving you now. I'm glad you made it back from the war boys. Remember what I told you about not trusting anyone. Please be safe and may God go with you." We hopped down out of the wagon and gratefully said goodbye to the farmer at his point of departure. "Good luck to you sir; Godspeed," I said.

Later that day, traveling by foot about ten miles north of Savannah, we saw a puzzling sight. From a distance, it appeared to be a Dray cart with the horse lying down and a frustrated soldier trying to get the horse to move. As we got closer, it turned out that our assumption wasn't even half right.

"How're you doing? Looks like you might need some help," I said to the soldier wearing a badly worn grey uniform but still sitting in the cart. I still could not clearly see his predicament.

"Not too well," he said in a strained voice. "I think my horse has died. He was old and the journey must have been too much for him. My name is Jonathan Walker. I served with General Cleburne at Franklin, Tennessee. I saw him go down too. He was a good soldier; a very good soldier. That was a terrible day for us. One I'll surely never forget."

"Yes, we knew of him. We were on duty that day at the Tennessee River guarding the wagon train. It's a damn shame. Many a good soldier was lost that day," I said.

"Too many," he replied. "A lot of them were my friends too. Grew up with them." He paused, "I'm trying to get home."

As I got closer to the wagon, I realized that Jonathan's legs were gone. "Wow," I said, startled by his deformed body and unable to control my thoughts. "I'm very sorry Jonathan. How did that happen?" I asked, trying to show sensitivity after my awkward response to what I was seeing.

"It's okay. I got them shot out from under me when we made the charge at Franklin. It was canister that got me. Damn effective it was. Sure stopped me in my tracks. I was lucky I didn't die. The doctor's told me later that I came very close to dying. At least I have my arms and some other important parts," he said with a dry smile.

"Where're you going?" Daniel asked.

"I'm trying to get back to my home in Savannah. It looks like it's going to take much longer now. It seems I may be crawling home. You do what you have to do though," he said with a matter-of-fact tone. "I learned that from the war."

"Maybe we can help. We're going that way too. Let me see if we can move your horse," Daniel said. "Oh, by the way, I'm Daniel and this here is my brother Micah."

With that, Daniel and I moved the dead horse away from the cart. To my astonishment, Daniel then picked up the two poles at the front of the cart and began to pull it. "Let's see how long I can do this before I collapse," Daniel said.

We then headed off in the direction of Savannah with me pushing from the back. Daniel and I traded spots every two miles or so and we eventually reached Savannah. There, on the edge of town, we were able to find some local boys who said they would help Jonathan get to his home.

"Micah, I want you and Daniel to have this," Jonathan said. "It's a Colt pistol I picked up at Franklin. It must have belonged to a cavalryman. It's all I have and I want you to take it."

"Jonathan, that's not necessary," I said.

"I want you to have it just the same. Here it's yours."

"Thank you Jonathan," I said, and reached out and took the pistol from him and tucked it under my belt.

"Thank you for your help guys and God bless you. You saved my life. I'll never forget you."

"No need to thank us Jonathan. I'm sure you would've done the same for us if the circumstances were reversed," said Daniel. "Maybe we'll see you again sometime when we come to the produce market in Savannah."

"I surely hope so. You'll always be welcome in my home," he said. "Oh, it's called the Wright House. It's on this road just inside town."

After leaving Jonathan, we started again on our journey home. We hoped to be there in a day or so. We were cautious about what we expected to find but we were greatly anticipating getting back to the farm. The comments made by the farmer earlier had worried us. Based on our recent experience with Cartwright and the devastation and sordid living conditions of the people we had seen as we traveled home, we knew the farmer was probably speaking the truth. We were soon to find out that things were even worse than we could've imagined.

Chapter 25

"We're getting closer Daniel. I can see the bend in the road just above our farm. It won't be long now."

"Yeah, I'm looking forward to seeing it again. We've been away a long time, too long. I'm worried that things are going to be very different now."

"Things can't be that much different, Daniel. We would have heard something, I'm sure. I'm hoping things aren't much different than the day we left. I expect Mother and Father are just a little bit older now, that's all. It's June, so they'll need us to help them with harvesting. Father may also need us to help with repairs on the house or barn."

As we turned the bend and looked toward the farm, we both froze. "Daniel, do you see that? Is that our farm? I don't recognize it. What's happened?" I went from a dead stop to a quick trot, then a hard run toward the farm with Daniel trailing me.

"My God, what's happened?" As we got closer, I yelled "Mother, father where are you?"

"We're over here," was mother's faint reply. I ran quickly over to where she was standing--next to what was left of our house. It had burned to the ground. Very little was left of what I'd remembered. Three of the four main walls of the house were now gone and I could see its foundation. I thought about the kitchen where mother had cooked our meals; the dining room where we had eaten and the bedroom where Daniel and I had slept and played while we were growing up. It was not a big house but it was comfortable—it provided shelter and living space for our family. It was our home. It was sad thinking about what it had meant to us, the memories made there and what remained of it now.

"Are you okay mother? Where's father?" I asked.

Mother then pointed over toward the barn. My eyes followed her arm as she slowly pointed in the direction of someone I barely recognized. I looked at him, but couldn't believe what I was seeing. He looked so much older. He appeared much lighter and frail than when I had left. His hair was much grayer than I remembered. His eyes were sunken and his skin was dark, wrinkled and weathered. He was also limping. He used a large stick for support as he walked toward us.

"What happened father? Are you okay?" I asked, as I looked at him. He looked back at me but didn't say anything.

"One of Sherman's raiding parties came through the area before Christmas. They burned our house, our barn, everything. They stole most of our animals. They didn't leave us much," mother said. "All we have left is the old tool shed out behind the barn and a few of the animals that we were able to find. We have some chickens, a few pigs but not much else."

"What about the other farms?" Daniel asked. "How about Aaron's farm? What about Aliyah? Is she safe?"

"Most of the farms were destroyed. Almost all had some damage," father said in a low saddened voice.

"Aliyah and Pearl are okay. Pearl went over to Aaron's farm or what's left of it this morning to see Aliyah. They're trying to get by just like we are. She should be home this evening. Boys, we're doing the best we can. We've been sleeping in the shed," mother said.

"We've got a lot of work to do, mother. We're going to help you rebuild. Don't worry. The farm will be bigger and better than before. Please don't worry," I said.

I then looked around, slowly. The house I was born in was razed to the ground. Our barn, where we used to milk the cows and store the feed and tools, was mostly gone. Fire had destroyed its roof and two of its sides. The farm was overgrown with weeds and grass and seemed badly neglected. Many of the pine trees near the house had also burned. Our home looked like many of the battered or destroyed farms and villages we had seen that were touched by the tragedy of war.

I was still hopeful, however. We were all alive so we had to be thankful for at least that. I was very happy about one other thing too. The large pecan tree in front of our house, where I had climbed as a young boy, had avoided the calamity that took place on much of the rest of the farm. As I had always been fond of pecans, this was a very a welcome sight.

"We have some awful news too. Aaron's wife, Eula was killed during the raid on their farm. She was trying to put out the fire on her house and died when a part of the burning roof fell on her. It was sad, very, very sad," mother said.

"Oh my God," I said. "How is the rest of Aaron's family? Are they okay? How is Aaron?"

"They survived. Only Eula was lost," father said.

"Are you boys okay?" mother asked, as she hugged Daniel again and seemed to be examining us as if to see if we were really here, alive and with all our limbs.

"We're fine Mother. I took a blow to the head several months back but I'm better now. Daniel's okay too. He got hit a few times but nothing serious, mainly scratches. You probably heard about what happened at Franklin and Nashville? Well, we were very fortunate that we weren't there. Those battles were awful for us. Many good Georgia boys were lost there."

"This whole war has been a tragedy. It never should have started. I knew that from the beginning. God has made us pay a horrible price for our stupidity," father said.

"Thank you Lord, for protecting my boys," mother uttered as she looked up toward a dark, overcast sky.

"We have a small garden out in the woods, by the pond. We cleared a small area last summer before the raid. We wanted to have something just in case," father said. "We were hearing about the war and General Sherman's army heading toward Atlanta. We hid as much as we could. It's lucky we did, because Sherman continued on to Savannah."

"Father, what happened to you? Why are you limping?" Daniel asked.

"He got hurt protesting Sherman's raiders as they ravaged our farm. One of the soldiers knocked him down, then trampled over him with his horse. He's lucky to be alive. He's lucky they didn't shoot him. They were terrible—dragons of the devil," mother said. "Spitting fire, venom and evil everywhere."

I looked at her. "Well, the war's over now mother. Daniel and I are back home. We all have our lives. We can rebuild the farm. We'll make it better, I promise. The war is just a horrible memory now."

Chapter 26

We'd been home working on the farm for several days when one morning I saw Daniel heading out to the dirt road in front of our house.

"Where're you going Daniel?"

"I'm going over to Aaron's farm to take a look around. I want to see for myself what's happened. I want to see how he's doing and offer my help."

"Mind if I go with you? I'd like to see him also." Mother had told us about Aaron's farm being destroyed and the loss of his loving wife Eula, during the raid. I wanted to see Aaron and offer my condolences for his losses. I sensed also that maybe Daniel wanted to see Aliyah. I must confess, I was curious about that.

"Sure. Come along," he said.

I knew it wouldn't be long before Daniel would try to see Aliyah again. It had been three long years that we'd been away and he hadn't heard much news about her during that time. We knew she was still at Aaron's farm. Mother had told us so. Aliyah probably decided to stay there after the war had ended. Many former slaves did just that. They stayed with their masters, not knowing how or having the confidence to survive on their own. Many had left their Plantations and farms only to come back after experiencing the economic and cultural realities of the post-war South.

The war was very cruel for soldiers in the way that it separated them from their families, friends and homes. It was even crueler still for the families of those who came back severely disabled or those who didn't return. Many had family members that were unaccounted for or missing. Had they run away, been killed or imprisoned? What did it mean when a soldier was missing? Many families didn't know and would never have a final accounting for their sons, husbands, fathers and uncles. Were they buried in an unknown grave with other unknown soldiers, hundreds of miles from home?

Daniel and I knew we had a lot of catching up to do with family and friends. Some of the news wouldn't be pleasant that was for sure. Since the end of the war, things had gotten much harder for them than before we left. We had changed too. How would we adjust to a normal life? We had seen so much violence and killing and needless destruction of property. How had that affected us?

Aaron's farm was about five miles down the road from ours. It was a warm, humid day but we made it there in a just over an hour. We had grown use to hot, muggy, tough marches during the war with a full load of equipment and this was nothing compared to that.

"It looks a lot like our farm," I said, looking toward Aaron's place and then toward Daniel.

He looked at me briefly and then looked back toward Aaron's farm. "Let's keep walking," he said.

We could see that the raiders had destroyed much of Aaron's farm also. His house and barn had been torched and no longer looked like what I had remembered. We could see that Aaron had begun to rebuild his house and barn but you could still see signs of fire. There was burnt timber and burned or scorched furniture scattered everywhere. Aaron had also started to rework his fields, though it was hot and humid and getting late in the season for some of the planting.

I glanced to the left and saw Aaron coming toward us from one of the fields near the wood line. He had an axe in his hand and it appeared he'd been chopping wood.

Daniel and I walked toward him. He seemed to recognize us and gave us a smile and a wave. Our pace picked up as we walked to get closer to him.

"Aaron, how are you? It's been a long time," I said, as I extended a hand to shake his.

He ignored my hand and grabbed me around the shoulders and pulled me close, in a strong, bear-like hug. He then turned his attention to Daniel and repeated the same. "We really missed you boys," he said with tears in his eyes. "We missed all the boys. I'm glad you're home safely. God, it's great to have you both home. Your mother always gave us the news when she received your letters. She was always so happy to hear from you. She was very worried you might not come back."

"Mother told us about Eula, Aaron. We're so very sorry to hear of it. You're in our prayers," Daniel said.

"I lost her before Christmas, during the raid. I was working in the woods, clearing land that day when they came and burned our house and barn. They messed up the fields too. Eula and the girls tried to put out the fire but the house collapsed. Eula was killed by falling timber from the roof. My girls did all they could but she didn't make it. I miss her so much. If only I had been there. Maybe I could have stopped them. I have so much guilt now. I should have been there for Eula."

"Aaron, we're so sorry. Eula was a good woman. Mother and father always talked very fondly of her. We'll all miss her," I said. I paused for a moment and then asked, "How is the rest of your family? How are Bella and Cassie? What about Jesse? Are they all okay?"

"Yes, thank God. Bella married a fellow a few months back. He was a soldier like you boys. His name is Strickland, Dan Strickland. She met him over in Savannah about a year ago. He lost an arm and was discharged. He's been helping me around the farm. He's a hard worker. I don't think I could've done nearly this much without him. He does more with one arm than many men can do with two."

"What about Cassie and Jesse?" I asked.

"Cassie's down the road with Aliyah. They went to get some water at the stream. Jesse is still out in the woods cutting trees. He's grown pretty big since the last time you saw him. He was with me the day the raiders came. I'm at least thankful for that or he might've been killed also."

"Hey, where's he going?" Aaron asked, pointing to Daniel, who suddenly had started walking away.

I turned around and saw Daniel walking down the road toward the stream. "I think he's off to look for Cassie and Aliyah. Aaron, we've been working hard every day with our father, helping to rebuild the farm but if you need any help with anything, please ask."

"Thank you Micah. I appreciate the kind offer."

"I'm going to go now and try and catch up with him. I'll see you soon," I said and turned, running off after Daniel.

I had just about caught up with him when I saw two figures coming up from the stream but still in the shadow of the woods. After a few moments, I could see that it was two women and I assumed one was Cassie and the other, Aliyah.

I watched closely as they came toward us, trying to get a better look at them. Cassie was about my age but I hadn't seen her in several years. She had long brown hair, was wearing a light-colored cotton dress and was slim in appearance. I remembered her as a skinny little kid, always running around the yard, playing hide-and-seek, when I was at Aaron's house. I never took much interest in her back then.

Aliyah looked much as I had remembered her. She had on a dark-colored, full-length cotton dress that buttoned down to her waist. It was probably given to her by one of Aaron's daughters, I thought. She was an attractive colored woman and easily carried a bucket of water in each hand. Her hair was up in a bun probably to keep her cool from the summer heat.

"Daniel, Daniel," I heard Aliyah scream. She put the buckets down and ran toward him. They hugged and clutched each other for several minutes. "You're home Daniel. You're safe. I was so worried about you," she said.

As I continued to look at them, I had forgotten about Cassie, who was coming toward us carrying one large bucket in her arms.

"Micah is that you?" Cassie asked.

"Yes," I said with a huge smile. "Wow, it's great to see you Cassie." As I gave her a big hug, I realized that she had become a beautiful young woman. I was pleasantly surprised by my new discovery.

"We just saw your father. We were very sorry to hear about your mother," I said to Cassie. "How is everyone doing now?"

"We're okay but we miss her a lot. We're trying to be strong for father and go on like she would've done. It's a tragedy, what happened to mother and the farm. We're doing the best we can to get along."

I looked over to my right and I noticed that Daniel and Aliyah were still hugging. "Aliyah, how are you? Can I have a hug too? It's been a long time."

"Sure can. Come here," Aliyah said and gave me a big welcome home hug also.

"We missed all of you," I said. "We missed the farm, our home. We're sure glad to be back."

With that, we started back toward Aaron's farm. It had been three long years and we had a lot of catching up to do. I was surprised by my attraction to Cassie. I felt a desire to get to know her better and spend more time with her. I could tell by the way that Daniel and Aliyah had hugged and continued to look at each other, that they too, had a lot more catching up to do.

Chapter 27

Father had sent Aliyah to live and work on Aaron's farm to separate Aliyah from Daniel. He felt their relationship was growing too close and that he needed to do something about it. Aaron had been aware of this from the beginning. Just looking at Aliyah now, three years later, it appeared that Aaron had been good to her. She looked healthy and her body was firm and muscular as I had remembered her. I reckoned that she had done chores around Aaron's farm much like her mother Pearl had done at ours.

"Micah, go over to Aaron's house and see if we can borrow his wagon. Ours was destroyed by them damn Yankees. Tell him I need to borrow it for a few days," father said. Aaron's wagon was still in decent condition since he had it with him the day of the raid and it had avoided the destruction that occurred on the rest of the farm.

I arrived at Aaron's farm about an hour later. After a few moments of friendly greetings and asking about the wagon, Aaron said to me, "You know Micah, Daniel's been over here several times to see Aliyah since you returned. I believe he still has strong feelings for her."

I looked at him for a moment and then said, "I don't think he ever stopped thinking about her while we were away. He didn't talk about her much but I knew she was always in his thoughts."

"Aliyah often asked about you and Daniel at dinner time. I gave her news when I had it. I treated her well Micah. I treated her as well as one of my own daughters."

"I know you did Aaron. I'm certain that Daniel believes that too."

"Do you think he loves her?"

"I believe he does."

"It's not right Micah. I'm not going to try to keep them apart but I don't think it's right. It's going to be tough for them. There are many around here that believe the colored's are the cause of all our troubles now. They're not going to feel very kindly to Daniel when they find out about the two of them. Things are bad around here now and people are looking to place blame wherever they can. You'd better warn him. I've heard of bad people riding around now, just looking for reasons to create trouble. Lord knows it's almost lawless around here anyway. There's no one who can prevent it either. Sheriff Copley is trying to keep the peace over in Savannah but he's in a different county. I'm afraid we're mostly on our own out here."

"Okay, Aaron. I'll speak with Daniel. I don't know if it will do any good but I'll speak to him."

A few days later, Daniel and I were working on father's barn. We stopped for a few minutes to get some water and rest, as it was very hot and humid.

"Daniel, I watched you hugging Aliyah the other day. Those didn't seem like just friendly, welcome back hugs. Do you still care about her?"

"Yes. We all care about her. We've known her all our lives. We grew up with her. We worked with her. She's like a sister to us. Of course I care for her."

"That's not what I meant Daniel. Do you love her?"

"Micah, it's none of your damn business, what I do or who I do it with. It's my business, not yours."

"I'm only concerned about you. The people here won't understand. They'll say things. They may even attack you. You're my brother, Daniel. We survived a brutal war together. We're very lucky to be alive. You know that. I just don't want to see you or Aliyah hurt."

"I can take care of myself and I don't care what the others think. Did father ask you to talk with me?"

"No, he didn't. He didn't say anything to me. I'm talking to you because you're my brother. I'm worried about you and Aliyah."

"Well don't be." Daniel dropped the hammer that was in his hand and walked away from me, toward the woods.

I knew I had hit a nerve with Daniel. I could see that he was upset. Maybe he was right after all. Maybe what he and Aliyah did together was their own business anyway. How could I judge my brother's behavior? It was not long after that however, that what Aaron had suggested and I had silently feared began to occur.

Chapter 28

It was a warm Sunday morning on a beautiful blue sky day when mother, father and I were walking leisurely to church which was just down the road from our farm. Although times were much tougher now than they had been before the war, my parents were very thankful at least that Daniel and I had returned home safely since many others had not. Our family's immediate prospects weren't great but we were hopeful that we could bring the farm back with perseverance and hard work and hopefully, in a few years, become self-sustaining again and maybe even begin to prosper.

"I'm looking forward to seeing our neighbors today and sharing thanks with them, to the almighty, for what we have and what he's provided," father said. He was always optimistic even in the toughest of times and surely the next few years would be a tough test for all of us.

"Yes, our boys came home from the war and we are very grateful for that. The good lord will help us take care of all the rest," mother said.

I was surprised by their positive comments. They had suffered so much during the war, as all of our neighbors had and would continue to suffer for many years to come. Yet I was comforted by what I was hearing. It seemed like they were ready to move on with their lives, to leave the past behind.

As we came upon the little white church with the tall reflective white steeple which was visible several miles down the road, the visual image was enhanced by a row of beautiful blooming pink crepe myrtles that could be seen dignifying the walkway into this place of worship.

The people in attendance that day were all suffering too but were determined to find the good and thank God for it. The war was over. People were down but not broken. I was optimistic for our church and community.

As the services were about to begin, those still outside walked in and took their seats on long wooden benches. The church was small and on this day, almost full. We began to sing a song, Rock of Ages to begin the service. We had just completed the first few verses when the congregation suddenly grew quiet seemingly, row by row. I saw others turning their heads to look back and then I heard father say, "Oh no." Mother groaned quietly and as I turned my head back to look toward the rear of the sanctuary, I saw the source of their discomfort. Aliyah and Daniel had walked in and had taken seats in the back row of the church. The building was now completely silent. I had this very uneasy feeling for several moments and then I saw the preacher move slowly down from the pulpit and walk toward the back rows where Daniel and Aliyah were sitting.

Reverend Jeremiah Walker had been a staunch confederate before the war and had given frequent sermons supporting the war. He was also one who interpreted the bible very strictly. Walker was a big man, in his early fifties with a full head of grey hair and bushy eyebrows. He had been a fisherman along coastal Georgia before joining the clergy, about fifteen years earlier.

He walked over to where they were seated and looked directly at Daniel. "We don't allow coloreds in our services young man," he said to Daniel in a low, brusque voice not even looking at Aliyah. "You know that. Please take this girl and leave our church."

"We're here to worship together with family and friends, preacher," Daniel said with a smile. "The Bible says God loves all his children, even those of a different color."

"I'm going to ask you to leave once more, Daniel. She is not welcome here. Please leave now."

Daniel looked from the Reverend to Aliyah and motioned with his head to come along. As they got up slowly and headed to the back of the church, I could see the color changing in Daniel's face. I had seen this before. He was like a volcano, building up pressure and getting ready to explode.

"Dam you preacher. Dam all of you. I hope you all burn in hell!" The congregation gasped as Daniel uttered those words. He and Aliyah departed from the church but less quietly than they had entered.

As they departed, the preacher directed a sharp look of disgust at my father then turned and started back to the front. After a few awkward moments, which seemed like hours to me, the congregation began to sing again. They continued where they had left off, with the same song.

It seemed so strange and ironic to me that later in the service, the preacher quoted biblical scriptures from the Gospel of Matthew, about how tax collectors and prostitutes would be welcomed into the Kingdom of God by believing in him. He had only minutes earlier dismissed Aliyah from the service, the sweetest, kindest and hardest working woman I had ever known. She was ordered to leave only because of her color. It didn't seem right to me, that this had just occurred in a house of God.

As we walked home from the service that day, we were mostly silent. I could see the look of stress on the faces of my mother and father. They were not the kind of people to share their feelings but I knew what they must have been thinking. Then, unexpectedly, father spoke up. "I've got to talk with Daniel. He doesn't realize where this is going. I have to stop him before someone else does."

Over the next few weeks, little was said about what occurred in church that day. I think we all had similar emotions, though unspoken. We all loved Aliyah but this was different. We knew that somehow, this relationship would have to end but we were concerned about what might happen to them if it didn't.

Chapter 29

As the days and weeks passed, Daniel became more and more aloof. He rarely talked or even looked at us when he was at the house. He dropped in for a meal every few days but that was about all we saw of him. If asked a question he would normally give a one word answer. I knew that if I wanted to talk with him, I was going to have to find him first.

Several weeks later on another warm Sunday afternoon, I decided it was time that I go find Daniel and talk with him. It was a lazy day for me anyway. I had attended church earlier in the morning and I was just sitting around the house reading a book and didn't have plans for much else. I knew that Daniel was building a small house for Aliyah and himself as he had mentioned it to me briefly a few days earlier. I wanted to ask him about it. I went out back behind the barn and found him fishing at a small pond that was close to our house.

"Daniel, where do you go every afternoon? You seem to just get lost."

"I'm working on something up where we used to play as kids."

"Really, what is it?"

"I started building my farm. We're going to need a place away from everyone."

"Do you mean you and Aliyah?"

"Yeah, that's right."

"Maybe I'll drop by one afternoon. I can give you a hand."

"Thanks for the offer little brother, but I'm doing just fine by myself."

"Well, I'll drop by in a few days anyway if you don't mind. I want to see how you're doing." He looked up at me then nodded his head. I was happy to even get that much approval from him.

A few days later I was headed that way. I didn't know exactly where he was building it but I knew the area where I needed to look. It was on our father's land at the very back of the property. The densely wooded area was still largely un-cleared. I remembered a small opening within the pine trees where we had played hide-and-seek when we were kids and I figured I should look there first. From the dirt road it was hard to find because of the close proximity of the trees to a barely visible animal trail leading into it. But it was there if you knew where to look.

Father had told us that when we returned from the war, he would give each of us property to start our own farms. Daniel was building on the land that father said would be his. They had not talked recently so I knew they hadn't discussed the issue of the land again, especially in view of recent events. However, father was not one to go back on his word even to force an issue of which he strongly believed.

The site was not very far from our farm, only about a half-mile down the road. It would be hard for a stranger to find however, and I was sure that's why Daniel had chosen that location. As I got closer, I wondered if I could still find it. I came to a place on the dirt road, where I thought the clearing should be. I left the road and walked slowly through a small opening in the trees. Walking gently, I was mindful of the rattlesnakes that also inhabited the area. After walking a short distance, I was pleasantly surprised to see the clearing straight ahead. I continued on the trail a little further and then saw where Daniel had been working. To my amazement, he had already completed three sides of a small house.

I saw Aliyah first and then Daniel. She was carrying some small logs over to where Daniel was cutting them. "Hi, Aliyah, hi Daniel, how're you doing?"

"We're doing just fine Micah. We're cutting wood for our house. How've you been?" Aliyah asked."

"I'm good. We're all good. I've been helping father with work on the farm. We're making good progress. Hopefully, we'll be done with it before the cold weather arrives."

"That's what I'm thinking about too, before the cold wind and rain arrives," Daniel said, seated on a tree stump not far from where I was standing.

I was surprised that Daniel even spoke. I figured I'd have to ask him questions just to get him to reply with one word answers just like at mealtime.

"It's good to see you Daniel. It's starting to look like a home. Can I help you?"

"No need. We're doing fine ourselves. Thanks anyway," Daniel said with a quick reply.

"Well, I didn't mean that you couldn't do the work by yourselves. I've known both of you long enough to know you can do almost anything that you decide to do. I'm just offering my help if you ever need it.

"Thank you Micah. That's very kind," said Aliyah.

"Daniel, do you remember that guy Cartwright who was at the stream when we were coming home from the war? The one who robbed us."

"Yeah. What about him?"

Well, I saw him a few weeks ago when I was in Savannah with Aaron. I saw Billy Dale with him too. I stayed out of view and I don't think they saw me but they're in town now. We need to be careful when we go there."

"I owe that Cartwright something and I plan to get even when I meet up with him again. If I do get my hands on him, I'm going to finish what he started that day at the stream. That man is bad. I never did like Billy either. He reminded me of a snake the way he used to sneak around camp just looking for trouble. What are they doing in town anyway?"

"Cartwright's probably been drifting since the war. I doubt he's got anywhere to go. I'd be surprised if anybody wanted him back. He must have followed Billy to Savannah. I think Billy has family just west of the city."

I looked at Daniel. "You know, we need to be careful. Cartwright's not going to give us an advantage if we run in to him again. It may even be better to try to avoid him if we can."

"I thought the war was over. What's all this talk about getting even?" asked Aliyah.

"Some things are never over. I want to meet up with Cartwright again that's for sure," Daniel said.

"Well if you do, you'd better be careful. That's all I'm saying Daniel. Be very careful."

I stayed a little while longer, talking about the family and then decided it was time to leave. I was hoping they'd ask me to stay and eat with them but they still had more to do before sunset. Besides, they were probably living off a few fish caught from the pond and a limited supply of vegetables. I really didn't want to ask. I knew that Mother was serving chicken and that was more to my liking.

"Aliyah, it was good to see you today. Daniel, do take care."

"It was good to see you too, Micah. Come again, anytime," Aliyah said. Daniel gave me a quick wave and then went back to sawing logs.

As I headed back toward father's farm, I thought about my chores for the next few days. I'd probably be working on the roof of the barn and clearing brush from where we'd be planting next spring. I thought about Daniel and Aliyah too--how much work they had already done and how I hoped things would work out for them.

I was also concerned about Cartwright and Billy Dale. I wondered if we would be meeting them again anytime soon. I knew that if there was any possibility for doing evil, they'd be the ones to find it.

Chapter 30

As summer marched into fall, I found myself thinking more and more about my neighbor's daughter Cassie. When I visited Aaron's farm, which was becoming more frequent, I would usually find her cooking, cleaning or taking care of the chickens near the house. I couldn't help but notice that she always seemed happy to see me in her own sarcastic way.

"Micah, are you here again?" she would often ask loudly and with a big grin on her face.

Cassie was about my age, twenty-five and had long brown hair and pretty green eyes. She was a little on the slender side and pleasantly attractive. Her naturally pale white skin was now deeply tanned from daily exposure to the summer sun. Her demeanor was always sweet and friendly, especially when I was around. She had remained unmarried during and just after the war as was often the case for southern women in rural communities due to the shortage of males and the number of widows resulting from the war.

"Are you staying for dinner Micah?" she usually asked, whenever I visited.

"I didn't come over here to be fed but if you have a little extra, I'd love to stay. Besides, I always enjoy your cooking."

"It's not a problem Micah. You don't eat that much anyway. That's why you're so skinny. You need to be eating more with all the work you've been doing lately. Come a little more often and I'll fatten you up."

"I know you're right Cassie but if I keep eating meals here your father's going to run me off."

I visited Aaron's house regularly over several months when one day my life changed forever. It was a totally unexpected occurrence that I should've seen coming.

"Micah, I need to go down to the stream and get some water for cooking. Will you come with me and help carry it back?" Cassie asked.

"Sure, I'll tag along and keep you company and maybe lend a hand too."

"I have my reasons of course," she said. "These buckets, when they're full of water, are very heavy and you're much stronger than me."

I quietly blushed remaining silent for a moment or two. "Well, I see that you only have two buckets. I think I can handle that."

When we got down to the stream, Cassie took off her shoes and sat down by the edge of the water. I sat down a few feet away from her on her left side. After putting the buckets into the stream and letting them fill, she lifted them out one at a time and placed them to her right. She then put her feet in the slow moving water of the stream and slowly, playfully, started to kick and splash the water. At first, her kicks were directed to the front but slowly she turned and begin splashing in my direction.

After a few moments observing her actions, I turned toward her and said, with a stern face and an uplifted eyebrow, "You'd better not get me wet."

"So what will you do about it if I do?" she asked. Cassie then made a big splash that soaked my pants and shirt.

"Now you're going to find out," I said and dove toward Cassie and the water, pulling her in and down on top of me.

She screamed as the water in the stream was cool and although shallow, she was almost totally submerged in it. "You've soaked me," she cried.

After a moment or two of laughter, I gently lifted her out of the stream. I put her on the bank but did not remove my hands, which were still wrapped tightly around her waist. She then gave me a kiss on the cheek. I paused, looking directly into her eyes and then gave her a quick kiss on the lips which then turned into one that lasted much longer than I could have anticipated. I was surprised and excited that she had responded so willfully.

We stayed down at the stream for about a half hour. We hugged, kissed and playfully joked with each other the whole time. "I think we'd better start heading back to the house," Cassie said. "Father will be worried if we don't return soon."

"It's going to take us a while to dry off. What are we going to tell your father? He'll be suspicious."

"I'll tell him I slipped into the water while I was filling the buckets and then you jumped in and pulled me out."

"I don't think your father's going to believe that but it's a good story I guess."

"Micah, don't worry. Father's not that naïve. He won't say anything, I'm sure."

It was at that moment as we walked backed to the house that I realized things were changing rapidly. My outlook and my life would be much better going forward and it would include Cassie.

Chapter 31

Early in the afternoon of a late fall day, several weeks later I was out in the field helping Aaron and Jesse clear some trees when I stopped what I was doing and walked over to Aaron. Jesse saw me standing next to Aaron and hollered jokingly in my direction, "Are you guys done for the day?"

"No Jesse. I'm just taking a break to talk with your father about something." I then looked back toward Aaron. "I just want you to know that I really enjoy being around Cassie. She's a wonderful person. I'm really very fond of her."

"Oh, are you really? I hadn't even noticed," he said with a grin on his face.

"I'm thinking about asking her to marry me."

Aaron looked at me and tilted his head slightly. "Well, how long are you going to think about it? Either you are or you're not. Which is it going to be Micah?"

"Well, yes sir. I want to propose to Cassie very soon. Maybe I will in the next few days. Can I have your blessing?"

"Of course you can. I welcome you, whole-heartedly into my family. I'll also give you some land to farm and to build a cabin for you and Cassie."

"Thank you. That is very generous. I want to discuss it with father also."

"Sure, I understand. But don't wait too long. Cassie will make someone a fine wife and I sure hope it's going to be you," he said with a smile.

I nodded and then walked back to where I was working. Over the next couple of days, I talked to both mother and father about my intentions. They were very fond of Cassie and happily approved.

On Sunday of the same week, at about three in the afternoon, I went over to Aaron's house and was greeted again by Cassie in her normal teasing manner, "Are you here again?"

"Yes I am." I paused, and then asked, "Well, are you going to ask me to stay for dinner?"

"You're always welcome Micah. You know that. Of course we want you to stay for dinner."

"Cassie. Will you take a walk with me down to the stream? I want to talk with you."

"What do you want to talk about?"

"Well, just come along with me, okay?"

"Alright, but I'll need to get back and make dinner soon. Father will be coming in from the fields soon and he'll be hungry."

We walked down the dirt road to the stream, just a short distance from the house. I found a nice grassy area near the water and sat down. It was the same location where Cassie and I had gotten soaked only a few weeks earlier. It was also the spot where we kissed for the first time. It was a pretty area with lots of Oak trees and abundant shade. We could hear the sounds of cheerful birds singing in the treetops.

"Cassie, please come sit here with me," I said and patted the ground next to me. "I was out in the field with your father earlier this week. Jesse was there also. We were clearing trees."

"Okay. So what happened?

"I told him I was going to ask you to marry me," I said nervously.

"You did? Well, what did he say? Did he say yes?" she asked with a smile.

"He gave me his blessing. Yes, he approved."

"Well, don't you think you should ask me also to get my approval?"

"Yes, I do." I then looked into her eyes and asked, "Cassie will you be my wife?"

She looked down at the stream, kicked the water with her foot, turned and looked at me and said, "Micah, I'll be happy to be your wife."

With that said and at that moment I must have been the happiest man in the county. I jumped up and yelled as loud as I could, "Yahoo."

Cassie looked at me and gave a big approving smile. She then got up and we embraced, kissed and hugged for what must have been ten minutes. It was the happiest day of my life.

"Micah, we'd better get back or father's going to come looking for us. He'll be worried."

"You're right but I really don't want to leave this place. I just want to stay here with you. I'm so happy. I haven't ever felt this way before."

"I know," said Cassie, "me too."

We then got up and started walking back toward Aaron's farm hand in hand. At that moment, nothing else going on in the world seemed to matter to us. We were very happy. Our hopes and dreams were now merging. We would be together, forever.

Chapter 32

Cassie and I decided to get married the third week in February. We knew it might be cold then but it would give us a little time before planting in March and continuing through the harvesting period in early to mid-summer. Reverend Walker agreed to conduct the service at Aaron's house, the home of the bride, which was customary at the time. Members of our church would be invited along with close family and friends. Afterwards, there would be a supper with everyone bringing their favorite dishes. It would be a happy time for everyone, getting together to celebrate and for the ladies to show off their cooking skills.

"I want to announce today, that two members of our congregation will be joining in holy marriage on Saturday, February 17th. Please plan on joining us for the marriage of Micah and Cassie at Aaron's house, at four o'clock in the afternoon. They ask that you bring one of your favorite dishes for the supper following this wonderful occasion," said Reverend Walker.

Cassie and I made a point of personally visiting many close friends and relatives in January, telling them our good news and announcing the upcoming wedding. They all seemed to be as excited as we were on hearing our happy news.

The wedding occurred on what turned out to be a very pleasant day especially for that time of year. The temperature had dropped a few days earlier which made us nervous but we had beautiful blue skies, bright sunshine and comfortably cool weather the day of the wedding. It was much different than the extreme heat we had only months earlier.

"Aaron, I was wondering if I might borrow your black coat. I need one for the wedding." I had noticed the coat that Aaron wore to church services many times and I thought that it might be appropriate for the wedding. "It may be a little big on me but coats are hard to afford these days. Father lost most of his clothes in the fire," I said.

"Micah, I will gladly loan you my coat. You may have to clean it up a little but otherwise, I think it's in pretty good condition; it only has a few small holes. I believe this will be the first time it's been used for a wedding though. I mostly wear it for Sunday services and funerals."

The week before the wedding, mother approached me after we had finished dinner. "Here, take this. It was your grandmother's wedding ring. I'm sure she would be happy knowing that you would give it to your bride," mother said. It was a small brass ring that had a little heart on it.

"Thank you mother, it's very pretty. I'll give it to Cassie as the symbol of my love for her."

Cassie wore a simple light brown dress for the wedding. It was one that her mother Eula, had worn on special occasions. She still missed her mother very much and this was her way of having her close by and in her thoughts on this special day.

The dress had long sleeves, a v-neckline and flowed gently to the floor. The lace was placed modestly at both the neckline and the end of the sleeves. With her long brown hair, Cassie looked angelic in that dress.

"You're so beautiful," I whispered in her ear as she stood next to me. "You must be an angel sent by God to be here with me."

She blushed, then said "Thank you, Micah. I feel wonderful and very special today. You've made me very, very happy."

Reverend Walker performed a simple ceremony. Cassie and I each exchanged our vows and then quickly, the ceremony was over. We were now married. I kissed my new bride and everyone applauded. I could see that my mother's eyes were teary and father was smiling proudly. I also noticed Aliyah and Daniel smiling at the back of the room. It was a very happy day for our families.

The meal following the wedding was special. It included turkey, ham, biscuits and several vegetables, cakes of many varieties, candy and fruit. Everyone seemed to enjoy themselves and most left the affair in good spirits and quite contented.

"Micah, you're getting a fine woman. Cassie will make you a good wife. God bless you both," said Reverend Walker. "I'll pray for your marriage, and for you to have long and healthy lives and many children."

"Thank you Reverend. Cassie and I feel very blessed."

Newly married couples from families of wealthier means might now be taking a long journey or trip to celebrate their marriage. They might travel and visit for several weeks a distant city such as Boston, Chicago or New York. Since my resources were meager, Cassie and I decided to stay a little closer to home and spend a few days celebrating and visiting in nearby Savannah which was an agreeable choice for both of us.

Cassie had never been away from home so she was eager to get started. There were things in Savannah that I wanted to show her and I knew we would have a wonderful time exploring the many gardens, parks and architecture of the city and tasting the great variety of southern food. Other than a brief trip with Aaron several weeks earlier, it had been almost four years since I had been there with the opportunity to explore the sights as a visitor. I was very anxious to see how the city was recovering from the harsh effects of the war.

Chapter 33

Cassie and I started our journey to Savannah a few days after the wedding. I asked Aaron if we could borrow his horse and wagon to make the trip.

"Sure you can, Micah. Just be sure to take care of my horse. He's getting old and I'm still going to need him for the planting season."

"I will Aaron. I'll take very good care of him. Thank you."

It took us a day, traveling by wagon, to reach Savannah. Although the roads were bumpy, dusty and strewn with holes, the weather for the trip was cool and sunny. Considering it was late February, we were grateful for the moderate temperatures and little rain.

Arriving in the city, we immediately began looking for a place to stay and stable our horse while visiting. We planned on being in Savannah for three or four days depending on what we wanted to do. Cassie and I were looking forward to eating some good Southern cooking, exploring the riverfront, viewing the beautiful homes and gardens while walking the city squares and anything else the city had to offer. When I was younger, I had traveled several times with Daniel and my father to Savannah and always found interesting things to do while father conducted his business.

The city of Savannah was designed and founded by General James Oglethorpe in the 1700's. Before the war began in 1861, Savannah was one of the most important cities in the South and also one of the prettiest in the Country. With its beautiful trees, carefully planned parks and squares, and lovely homes and architecture, it offered much to appreciate for those living in or visiting the city. A year earlier, before he headed north, General Sherman and his army had spent a couple of months in Savannah. He had spared the city from the devastation that other cities such as Atlanta and Columbia, South Carolina had not.

On Sherman's march to the sea, destruction was sown as he crossed Georgia from Atlanta to Savannah. Factories, bridges, railroads and farms were burned or destroyed and animals and food confiscated in foraging raids within a three hundred mile long and sixty mile wide swath. Anything that could benefit the Confederacy was destroyed or taken by the raiders. I wondered if Savannah showed any scars from the occupation and if it had recovered from the war.

"It's exciting to finally be here, Micah. You know, this is my first trip to Savannah. I've heard it's a beautiful city with charming houses and lovely parks," Cassie said. "I'm so happy to be here spending time with you. I can't wait to begin exploring."

"Me too, Cassie. I've also heard good things about Savannah. On my earlier trips, I didn't have much time to enjoy the city. I'm looking forward to seeing it with you." As we entered into town, I looked around curiously. I was hoping for the best, although I continued to wonder what we would find as a result of the war.

It was about five o'clock in the afternoon and getting dark when I stopped the wagon at what looked like a large boarding house. There was a small white sign with black lettering out front that read "Wright House." It looked like it might have been a large private home that was converted after the war. I imagined it to be an enviable family residence before the war but now being used to provide food and shelter for travelers. The house was surrounded by a white picket fence with crepe myrtle growing behind it. As we walked up to the entrance we saw rose bushes on both sides of the walkway. We had a mild winter so we were hopeful to see at least some flowers blooming early. Unfortunately, neither the crepe myrtle nor the rose bushes were blooming.

"This place must be beautiful during the spring. I can only imagine the flowers in full bloom," Cassie said.

We opened the door and walked inside. I really wasn't prepared for a big surprise. "Sir, we need a room for a few nights. Can you help us?" I asked.

A man reading a book, sitting on a chair by a small reading lamp in the corner of the room looked up at me and with eyes wide open said, "Well I'll be damned. Micah, is it you?"

"Yes, I'm Micah. But sir, I'm having trouble remembering you." I then glanced down and noticed that the man didn't have legs. "Oh my God. You're Jonathan Walker aren't you? God bless you. It's so great to see you again. How are you doing?"

"That's right Micah. It's me. You and your brother helped me along the road when I was returning home from the war. You helped me get back to Savannah. I probably wouldn't have made it if it hadn't been for you and Daniel that day. But you saved me. I'll never forget you. I owe you my life."

"Oh, excuse me Jonathan. This is my wife, Cassie. We were married just a few days ago and we've come to visit your city."

"I'm much honored to meet you Jonathan," Cassie said. "Micah has mentioned you several times. He wondered how you were doing. We're glad to see you're doing so well."

"No, please, the honor is mine and congratulations to both of you on your wedding." Jonathan then looked at me and then back to Cassie. "Micah and Daniel stopped to help me when no one else would. The others who passed by must have thought I was too far gone to be helped. I believe I would've died right there on that dirty, dusty road if Micah and Daniel hadn't come along. I owe them plenty."

"You would have done it for us, Jonathan. We only did what was right." I paused. "Well, enough of that talk. What about your city? Has it changed much since you were away?"

"It's a lot different now than before the war. All the slaves that were freed, well, many have flooded into our city. Many followed Sherman's army when he came here. Some have found work cleaning streets, digging ditches, repairing roads and working at the docks but many don't have any skills and are crowding into shanty towns around the city. Those places are hardly livable—there's little food or clean water and they're filthy. The area is ripe for disease. People are dying down there. I don't know what we're going to do Micah. We can't handle them all. They don't even have proper shelter from the weather. There are too many of them. They're living in the streets, in the alleys, anywhere they can find. Wild dogs are roaming around down there also. It's hard to see, Micah. You'd better avoid those areas while you're here. They're just not safe."

"Well, we've just come into town and we're looking for a place to stay. Luckily, yours was the first place we found. We need a place to rest and stable our horse. Can you give us shelter for a few days?"

"Sure Micah. I have a nice room I can give you and Cassie and we have a stable around back. This house belongs to my family. We've had it for several generations going back before the war. You can stay here and have meals with us for the time you're in Savannah. There'll be no charge. I owe it to you Micah. I'll tell you the areas to visit, things to see and you'll be safe while you're here."

"Thank you Jonathan. We appreciate your hospitality but we mean to pay you."

"Please Micah. After what you did for me, I would be insulted if you tried. You're my guest while you're here in Savannah."

"Well, thank you again Jonathan."

"I'll give you and Cassie room four, which is just up the stairs and down the hallway. If you want to get cleaned up, rest a little and then come back down, we'll be having our evening meal at six." He looked at both of us and said with a smile, "Let me know if you need anything. It's so great to see you again Micah and to meet you Cassie."

"Thank you Jonathan. This house is so lovely. Micah and I will be very happy here."

We were tired from our journey but we wanted to get cleaned up and have supper. It was great seeing and talking with Jonathan today. What a wonderful surprise. Looking around Savannah could wait until tomorrow. We didn't know what the next day would bring but we were excited to get going and start looking.

Chapter 34

The next morning Cassie and I got up early, had breakfast and headed out to explore Savannah. As we started out the front door we saw Jonathan sitting on a chair on the porch reading a newspaper.

"You're a few weeks early to see the azaleas blooming but you might see some camellias today. They're my favorite blooming flower anyway. You may see them in gardens today as you pass by the houses. Remember Micah, stay away from those shantytowns. They're very dangerous. Also, watch out for wandering bands of men, both white and Negro. Some of them are just looking for trouble. You'll be safe if you stay in the better parts of town."

"Okay. Thanks Jonathan. We're anxious to explore your city. We'll be back later this afternoon."

As we left the Wright House, I thought about how lucky we had been to find Jonathan and his family's home. It had been almost nine months since Daniel and I had helped Jonathan that day on the road. We wondered what had happened to him after we dropped him off in Savannah. It was good to see him and I couldn't wait to tell Daniel on our return home.

As we walked along on our exploration, we saw the beautiful squares next to oak tree lined roads. Each square was different and most had benches where you could sit and view the surroundings. Some of the benches were made of wood and others of wrought iron. We were told that Sherman's soldiers had made camp in the parks over a year ago and had damaged them and the gardens during their occupation. It was obvious to us that much work had been done since because what we saw was beautiful.

"In the cemetery, soldiers created mischief by mixing up headstones of the deceased and some of them even used dug-up coffins for personal shelters," said one of the local residents as we were walking near the cemetery. "It took a lot of work to put those misplaced back where they belonged."

As we were walking along hand-in-hand viewing the sights, we decided to pause for a while and sit down on a bench in one of the parks we were passing through. It was covered in shade by large live oak trees with the hanging Spanish moss. The birds were busy going about their business and chirping as they worked. It was a cool, sunny day and quite pleasant to be outdoors.

"What a beautiful day it is today, Micah," Cassie said, as she looked around, stretched out her arms and took a deep breath of fresh air. "I'm excited to be here. This is the first real city I've ever visited."

"Well, we'd better get up and start walking then or we may miss something. There's still a lot left for us to see."

Most of the morning and early afternoon was spent browsing leisurely through the parks and looking at the beautiful homes along the tree-lined streets. We stopped several times to look at the scenery and to have the lunch we had brought with us.

We were about ten blocks away from the Wright House when we noticed a commotion at one of the street corners ahead of us. From a distance it looked like several men fighting. As we got closer however, we could see that it was several white men beating up a teenage Negro boy. After a few moments, I saw the boy jump up from the ground and run away in the opposite direction from where we had come.

I wanted to be cautious but we continued walking slowly toward the location where the fighting had occurred. As I got closer, I thought I recognized a couple of the aggressors.

"Billy Dale," I yelled out. One of the fellows in the group of white men turned and looked over toward me, then started coming in my direction.

As he came closer to us, he said "Do I know you fella?"

"Billy, its Micah from the 54th. I thought I recognized you. We saw a commotion and wondered what was going on."

"Micah, I haven't seen you since North Carolina. How the hell are you? I guess you made it back to your farm okay," he said.

"That's right. Daniel and I made it back safely, thank goodness. What was that all about?" I said and pointed over to where the fighting had just taken place.

"Not much really. We caught a Negro boy over where he shouldn't have been and wanted to teach him a lesson. We beat him up pretty good too, I think. We didn't want to kill him but just teach him a lesson so others will learn not to come down this way. They'll learn to stay in their own areas and away from here."

"Well, he looked to be mighty scared and limping when he ran off. I think you did what you wanted to do. Who are those others with you?" I asked, pointing back to the men.

"The tall fellow on the left is named Cartwright and the other guy next to him is Evans. I met them a few months back. Both of them were soldiers with us under Hood. They were in the Cavalry. We've been hanging out together here in Savannah. We're organizing a group and we're looking for others to come join us. I'll come visit you in a few weeks so we can talk," he said. "I know about where your farm is located. It's just southwest of here, isn't it?"

"Yeah, but when I get back, I've got to get busy farming again. There's lots of work to do. We're coming up on the planting season. Sherman's raiders set us back though, like others in the area. Most of the farms were either damaged or destroyed. It's going to take a lot of work to get back to where we were before the war."

"I'll come see you anyway, Micah. Maybe I can interest you in what we're doing here."

"I don't know Billy. I'm a farmer." I paused for a moment then said, "We need to get going. I'll see you later," and we began walking away, back in the direction of the house.

"Give it some thought, Micah. With your army experience, you can help us. I'll be visiting you in a few weeks. You can count on it."

I looked back at Billy again and gave a slight nod. After we were about a block down the road, Cassie said, "Those are evil men, Micah. Why do they need you anyway? Do the Devil's work I bet. I think you'd better avoid them, that's for sure."

"I don't know what they want, Cassie. I think you're right though. I suspect they're up to no good. When I get back to the farm, I need to talk with Daniel about this. I think those guys are going to be trouble for everyone. Did you see that tall guy, Cartwright that Billy mentioned? He was one of the guys who stopped us when we were coming home. They robbed us at gunpoint but we didn't have much for them to take. I'm afraid that if Daniel had been with us today, he would've wanted to settle the score with Mr. Cartwright right then and there. Let's head back to the house now. We can rest a little bit and then wash up for supper."

"I don't like them," Cassie said. "They're evil. I don't want you to join any group that they're organizing."

"Don't worry Cassie. They don't have anything I want or need." As we neared the Wright House, I wondered when I would be seeing Billy again and what he could possibly want from me. I also knew that I had to find Daniel and tell him what I'd seen.

Chapter 35

After spending several days in Savannah, it was time for us to head home. "Jonathan, we've enjoyed our time here. You've made us feel very welcome. Thank you for taking such good care of us. Please come and visit the farm if you're ever over our way," I said.

"I'd love to Micah, if I can ever get away. As you've seen, I stay pretty busy running the house and all. I'm glad your visit went well. You're always welcome here whenever you come to the city. Have a safe journey home." He then looked at Cassie. "It was great meeting you. I hope to see you again soon."

"Thank you Jonathan. We've enjoyed our stay. It's so lovely here," Cassie said.

As we left town, we passed Forsyth Park and the pretty white fountain. "This park is beautiful, Micah. I hope we can come back and visit again."

"I'm sure we will Cassie. But now I'm ready to go home. As we began our return trip on the dry dirt road, we knew we had a lot of work ahead of us. We wanted to get started building our home and farm and helping our parents' with the upcoming planting season.

The trip back was quiet and uneventful except that one of the wheels came off and it took me some time and muscle to put it back on the wagon. Because of that, our trip home took two days rather than the one it took us to get to Savannah. We were cautious with the wagon going home, traveling slowly on the bumpy roads.

We decided to stop off at my parent's house first, to visit mother and father. I wanted to tell them about our trip and see how they were getting along. It was the closest of the farms on our way back.

As I went into the house it seemed strangely quiet and I wondered why. Were they outside working I wondered? I then saw mother near the kitchen area. She looked tired and sad.

"Mother what is wrong. Are you sick?"

"No, but your father is. He's come down with a bad fever and Doctor Reed doesn't think he's going to make it. He's been sick for several days. The fever started the day you left."

"I'm so sorry mother, what can we do?" Cassie asked.

"I'm afraid all we can do now is pray," mother said.

I walked past Pearl, who was standing outside my father's room and walked in to where he was laying.

"Father, we just got back and heard that you're sick. What can we do for you?"

He looked pale and his eyes were halfway opened. He felt very warm to the touch as I bent down and clutched his hand. I could see a rash on his lower chest. He turned his head slowly toward me and said in a low voice, "Micah, thank you for stopping. It's good to see you. I'm afraid I'm going to be leaving soon. Please take care of your mother for me."

"I will father. But keep fighting. You'll get better, I know you will."

He then closed his eyes and turned his head. I got up slowly, turned and walked out of the room. I was quickly overcome with a deep sadness.

"He'll soon be in a better place Micah. He'll be with the Lord," Pearl said.

About two days later, father passed away. Doctor Reed said that he had Typhoid fever. We buried him in a simple wooden coffin, in the little cemetery next to the church. It was a pretty area on a small hill, surrounded by pine trees. Father would've been pleased, I thought. He was now with family and friends who had preceded him.

Everyone in the community came out for the service. Father had led a tough farm life, had worked very hard for many years and was well respected. He would be missed.

"He was a good man—a good farmer and a good servant of God," Reverend Walker said. "He worked so hard and endured so much in this lifetime; he deserves now to have peace in heaven. We will all miss him. Our thoughts and prayers go out to his family he leaves behind."

Daniel and Aliyah were at the service. I walked over to where they were standing, looked at them and gave them a soft smile.

"We'll miss him Daniel," I said. He always meant well even when his decisions were hard for us to understand."

He nodded. "Yes, we will. I'll remember the lessons of life he taught us."

Daniel then turned and walked away from father's gravesite, over to a big oak tree standing nearby. I saw the tears in his eyes as he passed by me.

Aliyah leaned over toward me and whispered in my ear, "Daniel made peace with your father before he passed. Your father treated me mostly well, Micah. I will miss him too."

I looked over at mother and wondered how she could go on without him. She looked so sad and lost at this moment. I had never seen her this way before. Maybe we should all live together now, I thought. I knew we needed to be there for her at this difficult time.

As we walked away from the cemetery, I thought back to all the good times we had with father, especially before the war when Daniel and I were just young boys. I remembered how he had taught us to hunt and fish. He had even taught us to swim in the Altamaha. I also thought about how things had changed since then-- the war, Daniel's relationship with Aliyah and the hard times we were now facing. I knew there was much work ahead of us. I knew that life would continue to be a struggle but we had to go on. There would be good and bad times ahead. I also thought about my life with Cassie and I was very optimistic about that and our future family.

Chapter 36

One day late in March, I was busy planting in the fields when I saw a blurry figure riding down the road toward me on horseback at a slow trot. I didn't recognize him at first but as he got closer, I could see that it was Billy Dale. He had now found me I thought to myself and was coming to talk to me about something. I didn't have any idea what he wanted to talk about but I didn't think I wanted to hear it anyway.

As he got closer, his horse slowed and he hopped down to the ground about ten feet in front of me. I dropped the rake I held in my hands and moved over to greet him.

"Hey Billy, what brings you out this way?" I asked, with my hands firmly on my hips, choosing not to make the effort to reach out and shake hands with him.

"What do you think, Micah? It feels like it's getting hot a little early this year and I sure could use a drink of water. The road getting here was dusty and filled with ruts. It was hazardous for my horse too."

"Here, have some water from this jug. I just filled it a little while ago. It should still be cool."

"Do you remember Micah, after a long road march the regiment would stop by a slow flowing stream surrounded by large shady trees? That cool water was so refreshing. I can still taste it now. How 'bout you?"

"Yeah, but I also remember some really cold days Billy, when the streams were frozen and we had to melt the ice just to get a drink of water. If you'll remember, we even had to do that to get the horses to drink. There were some good times and bad times on those marches as I remember it."

"You're right. I remember those days too, Micah. It wasn't so long ago. A lot has changed since then, don't you think? Nothing is the same anymore. Things have gotten much worse since before the war."

"Maybe it has. All I know is that I've been working out here in the fields in this heat for several days now and I haven't had much time to think about the war. I just work hard and try to ignore the weather. I guess I'm just used to the heat now. I've got to get this planting done soon or we won't have anything to harvest this year. I'm behind and I'm trying to catch up now. My father passed a few weeks back and I'm doing most of the work by myself now. I need to get the planting done and have a good harvest so I can start paying off some of our debts."

"Sorry to hear about your father," he said then paused. "Micah, I want to talk with you about something. You saw all those Negroes in Savannah a few weeks ago didn't you? Well, it looks like their trying to take over the place. Ever since Lincoln freed them, they don't want to do what their supposed to do anymore. They want to be paid now to work the same fields they were working a year ago and work less hours each day too. Now there's even talk of teaching them to read and write. We can't let that happen, Micah. Do you understand? We need to put them back in their place. We need to restore things to the way they were before the war."

"How're you planning on doing that Billy? It doesn't sound to me like it'll be easy or even legal. It sounds like there could be trouble. The war's over. I'm not looking for any more trouble."

"Well, this is what we white folks have to do now. We need to protect ourselves and our families. We have to keep them in their place. Maybe we need to visit some of these so called teachers too. I hear they're coming down from up North somewhere. Boston, I hear. I think we need to talk with them and maybe scare them a little. Maybe they'll leave if we can convince them we don't want them down here. Hell, maybe they'll even stop coming. What do you think Micah?"

"I don't think it's anything I'm interested in doing Billy. I'm a farmer. I'm not a crusader for causes. I need to be here taking care of my farm and family. I don't have time to be scaring Negroes or teachers. I've got lots of catching up to do right here on this farm. Besides, I'm a churchgoing man. What would my preacher say if he knew I was involved in something like that?"

"Well, hell Micah. Most of the preachers in these parts feel the same way as I do. They're not going to say anything to you. They're probably going to pat you on the back. Maybe even thank you."

"I don't think so Billy. I just don't have time for that now."

"We're organizing Micah. We just need your help once in a while; maybe even just at night. There's quite a few in Savannah that have already joined us. Even some of the Generals have joined the cause. They understand the importance of this matter. You need to come join us Micah. We're going to be doing something and we're going to be doing it soon. Can I count on you to be there when we need you?"

"Billy, I said I'm not interested. I've got too much work to do right now. I don't have time to be worrying about Negroes and teachers. I've put down my musket and picked up a rake. I'm a farmer now. That's the way it's got to be."

"Okay Micah. I'm telling you though, we're going to be doing something and I hope you'll change your mind. Hey, what about your brother, Daniel? I'm sure he probably wants to deal with those Negroes too. Where is he anyway?"

"I don't think so Billy. He's busy planting now just like me. We've got a lot of work to do around here and we don't have much time for anything else. Billy, we can't help you."

"Well, I'm sorry to hear that. You take care of yourself now. You tell Daniel that I asked about him. We sure could use you boys. We need good foot soldiers. Just think about it, okay? Come see me in Savannah if you change your mind, but don't wait too long. We need your help now."

"I need to get back to work. Billy, you take care."

As he got back up on his horse and started to ride away, I looked back slowly at him. I thought about how bad things had become. Life did seem to be much more difficult now than it was before the war. Things had changed but I had too much to do on the farm and no time for Billy's mischief. I also wondered if things were about to get worse. Billy Dale always seemed to have a way of causing trouble and it seemed like he was getting involved again in something of which I didn't care to participate.

Chapter 37

"Cassie, I'm going to see Daniel. Do you want to come?"

"Yeah. I want to see Aliyah also. It's been a few weeks. I want to see how they're doing. I hope everything's okay over there."

As we walked down the road through the piney woods and to the clearing where Daniel and Aliyah were building their house, I noted the improvements they had already made. It looked nearly complete now with all four walls, a roof and a modest porch. Also, I noticed that some of the adjacent fields had been cleared of pine trees and brush. I hadn't been there for a while but I shouldn't have been surprised. When Daniel set his mind to do something, he usually got it done and quickly.

"Daniel, Aliyah, anyone home?" I called out. After several calls and hearing no answer, I said to Cassie with a puzzled look on my face, "I wonder where they are. Let's walk to the pond. Maybe they're down there."

As we got closer to the pond, I noticed two figures sitting by the water. The area by the pond was heavily shaded and I couldn't tell if it was them or not. I had only been back to that pond a few times in recent years. However, when Daniel and I were young, if we weren't playing or fishing down at the river, this is where you would normally find us.

"Hey Daniel, hi Aliyah, how's the fishing?" I asked.

Daniel looked up to see who it was. He and Aliyah then got up and came over to us. They both gave Cassie a big hug first, then me. "We're fine but the fishing's slow today. It's been so damn hot lately that I'm sure the fish have had lots of bugs to feed on. They're not acting very hungry today."

"We've been trying to catch them but they're not biting. Daniel says they're in there but I only got one nibble and it was from a big old catfish. I think he's way too smart to get caught by us. He must have told his friends too," said Aliyah.

"I know they're in there. Daniel and I always used to bring fish home for mother to cook. You just have to be patient. If you dangle something in front of them long enough, their curiosity will get the best of them and they'll bite." I looked over at Daniel. "Can I talk with you about something?"

"Yeah, sure, let's go over there by that tree stump."

"Cassie, will you stay with Aliyah while I talk with Daniel. Maybe she'll let you try your luck at fishing. We'll be back in a little bit."

As we neared the stump I looked at Daniel and said, "Billy Dale came to visit me a few days ago."

"Who came to visit you? You mean that little snake from our unit is around here? He'd better not show his face around me."

"Not only that but he's joined up with that fellow Cartwright. Do you remember him?"

"Yeah, I do. I'd really like to meet up with that asshole again. So what are those vermin up to?"

"They're organizing a group to harass and scare the Negroes in Savannah; maybe the friendly white folk too. Remember, I told you about all the Negroes I'd seen in Savannah? Many of them had followed Sherman there when he captured the city back in sixty-four. Others left their farms and plantations and have journeyed there. Well, Billy and his group are organizing to do something about it. I think they aim to scare the Negroes and maybe even do something worse. If Billy Dale and Cartwright are involved, it means something bad is going to happen, you know that."

"Where are they now Micah?

"Billy told me that if I was interested in joining up with them, to come to Savannah. He asked about you too. I told him that neither you nor I had the time or interest. I told him you were busy farming just like me."

"It's a good thing he came to you and not me because I would've beat his ass. I never did like him. That guy Cartwright, I'd shoot him. He's nothing but a hooligan, a criminal. I would definitely shoot first and not ask what he wanted."

"Well, I hope it doesn't come to that Daniel but I thought you should know. I do believe that bad things are about to begin around here and I hope we can avoid the trouble. I really thought that after the war all the violence was over."

"Thanks Micah. Let's go back and see how Cassie and Aliyah are doing."

"Caught any fish yet?" I asked, as I looked at Cassie.

"No, but Aliyah did. She caught a couple of small ones. They're in that bucket. Maybe we can catch a few more and have dinner this evening?"

"That sounds good, Cassie. We've been looking forward to seeing you and Micah. It's been too long. I'm going to walk back to the house to get a fire started. Come along when you're done fishing," Daniel said.

"Alright Daniel. The way Aliyah is working those fish now, we should be back to the house pretty soon."

We had a good visit with Daniel and Aliyah that day. Times were tough but we were still able to eat enough fish and vegetables to fill an empty stomach. After dinner, we helped clean up, told a few fish stories and then walked back in the dark to mother's house. There was much work left to be done the next morning and I needed to get an early start.

Chapter 38

The remainder of 1866 was peaceful and happy for us. Farmers in the area continued to eke out a minimal existence by their resourcefulness, hard work, helping their fellow farmers and the generosity of a few merchants willing to risk giving the seed and tools necessary to make even modest gains on our farms possible. We planted cotton, corn and other vegetables that we sold at market and some of which we kept for our own use to get us through to the next year. Also, extra effort was needed to increase our animal populations and their productivity. Weather and disease were a continuing threat with which we had to deal.

There were however, two important family events occurring later in the year that made us all very happy. The first was the marriage of my mother to our neighbor Aaron. Aaron's wife, Eula had died after the Yankee raid on his farm and he had been living alone with his son Jesse since his daughters departed. He was lonely and needed someone to share his remaining years with him.

"Micah, Aaron has asked me to be his wife. I think it would be very good for both of us. How do you feel about that?"

"I think that's wonderful mother. I like Aaron. He's been very good to both Cassie and me. He's a good farmer, he loves his family and the land and I believe he would treat you very well."

"He wants me to come and live with him on his farm. You and Cassie can stay here and farm this land. I think the marriage will be good for both of our families. He's a good person, with good religion. I believe it's the right thing for me to do. I think your father would approve too."

"That makes me very happy mother. I will talk with Cassie. I know she'll be as happy as I am."

The ceremony was simple and performed by Reverend Walker. Aaron and mother were about the same age and both had recent losses. The match was good for everyone. It was a very joyous occasion.

The second event was the birth of our daughter Ella. She was a very blessed surprise for both Cassie and me.

I was out working in the field one day when I saw Cassie walking over toward me. "Micah, will you walk down to the stream with me? I want to discuss something with you."

"I'm busy planting corn right now Cassie. Can it wait a bit?"

"No Micah. I can't wait. I need to talk with you now."

"Okay, I'm coming," I said and dropped the shovel on the ground next to where I'd been working.

As we walked down the road toward the stream, Cassie grabbed my hand and held it very tight. "Hey, be careful with that hand I'm going to need it later," I said. I could see that she was beaming with excitement. I knew she had something to tell me and I knew it would be good--I just didn't have any idea what it could be.

"Micah, do you remember that I was going to see Dr. Reed this morning at father's house? Father's been having problems with his back and Dr. Reed stopped over to see him."

"Yes, I did know that, though I forgot the reason you were going. Are you okay? You said you were going to see him but I don't remember why."

"We're going to have a baby, Micah." Cassie paused for a moment to see my reaction. "Doctor Reed said the baby will arrive before the end of the year."

I was so excited, so caught off guard that I could hardly reply. Speechless for the moment, I grabbed her and gave her a big hug. "Cassie, that is so wonderful! I'm so happy! How do you feel? Are you okay?"

"I'm fine Micah. The doctor says I'm doing well. He told me to take it easy though and not try to do too much before the baby comes."

"We have to think of a name. How about Jonah? What about Jacob, after my father?"

"Micah, we don't even know if it will be a boy or girl yet. We can think about names later. We'll pick out one by the time the baby arrives."

Pearl was still living in our house after the war. She had not departed as many former slaves had on other farms and plantations. Many had fled when Sherman passed through Georgia in 1864. Others had left after the war ended in 1865. Pearl asked if she could stay and mother said that was fine. I think part of the reason Pearl wanted to stay was so she could be close to Aliyah. Aliyah had chosen to stay I assumed because of Daniel.

"Pearl, you know that you don't have to stay here any longer. You're free to go at any time. I've known you my entire life and care for you very much but we can't force you to stay here any longer. You know that don't you?"

"I'm here because I want to be Micah. Where am I going to go anyway? Your family is my family too. I want to be here. We've got a lot of work to do to get this farm back on its feet. And, you need to fix this leaky roof," she said, pointing to an area above her head.

"You're right of course. I still have a lot of work to do. I don't have any time to waste." I paused, "I'm happy you're here."

Pearl was very helpful as we waited for our baby to be born. She was able to pick up the slack and help Cassie during that demanding period. We were very grateful that Pearl had chosen to stay with us and we told her so on many occasions.

"You have a beautiful baby daughter," Dr. Reed said. "Both mother and daughter are doing fine, Micah. You take care of this family. They need you more than ever now."

"I will doctor. Thank you so much."

We named our daughter Ella. I had suggested the name to Cassie after an angelic nurse I had met near a field hospital outside of Atlanta, back in sixty-four. She was so caring and loving for the sick and wounded that it made a strong impression on me. She would comfort them by holding their hand and gently singing to them. For many, it was time spent with an angel in their final hours here on earth.

Ella was beautiful, with reddish blond hair, soft rosy cheeks and big beautiful blue eyes. She was so full of life and curious about her new world even at that early age. She was such a wonderful addition to our family. As the months moved past and Ella grew, we couldn't ever have imagined our lives without her.

As I look back now, the year ended well for us. Mother's marriage to Aaron and the birth of our daughter, Ella were the events that made it so special for us. The farm was starting to become productive again and we were optimistic about what lay ahead.

Chapter 39

Early in the spring of 1867, Daniel and I departed for Savannah to pick up farm supplies. We planned on visiting with Jonathan also as Daniel had not seen him since returning home at the end of the war. Jesse came along with us to pick up some items for Aaron.

We pulled the wagon over, stopping out front as we arrived at the Wright House. We tied our horse to a post, walked in to the house and called out for Jonathan.

"Jonathan isn't here right now. He went down to the river to buy fish. He'll be back later this afternoon," a Negro woman, cleaning on the porch called back to us. "Stop back later."

"Yes we will," I said. "We'll be back later this afternoon. Please tell him that Micah and Daniel stopped by to see him. He'll know who we are."

We then climbed back into the wagon and headed down toward the river to buy supplies. Our wagon moved slowly along the bumpy road filled with numerous holes made worse by recent rains and those who had traveled this way before us.

Up ahead, we saw a group of men standing by the side of the road next to an old warehouse. They seemed to be talking and joking with each other. As we got closer, I silently identified a couple of the men that were standing there. Suddenly, I had a sick feeling stirring deep within my stomach.

"I'll be damned," I heard Daniel say quietly and then he leaped out of the wagon and charged directly toward the unsuspecting men. We were only about hundred feet away from them at that point. Daniel went straight for the taller man, who I recognized as Cartwright. Daniel grabbed him violently, threw him against the wall and then punched him repeatedly about the head and face.

I jumped out of the wagon and ran over to where Daniel was attacking Cartwright. Daniel continued to beat up on Cartwright as the men surrounding them tried to pull them apart. Cartwright had been caught totally off guard by Daniel, unaware of the surprise attack and appeared to be taking a severe beating.

Others jumped in then and separated them as I got there. I could see blood covering and dripping down from the face of Cartwright. His lip was badly cut and he had a large swelling lump on the right side of his forehead.

"Daniel, stop" I hollered repeatedly, jumping into the middle of the fight with the others and trying to restrain Daniel who was still swinging his fists at Cartwright. He continued to swing crazily until he was subdued and forced to the ground.

"That guy's crazy," someone yelled. I turned my head and saw that it was Billy Dale. "Get the Sheriff," he hollered.

Several minutes later, Sheriff Ben Copley came running up toward us. He was a big man in both height and weight, in his mid-forties and had a long, bushy mustache. He was breathing heavily from his labored run.

With Daniel now restrained by the group, the Sheriff asked, "What's going on here? Why are you fighting in my town?"

"That guy should be in jail Sheriff," said Cartwright, holding his beat-up jaw. "If you don't lock him up, I'll kill him right here and now," he said, as he moved his hand down toward his gun.

"Calm down now. Nobody's killing anyone here today. Take your hand away from that gun, Cartwright or I'll be taking you along too. I'm taking this man back to the jail," said Copley, looking at Daniel. "You guys break it up now. Move on. I don't want any more trouble here today."

The Sheriff then started walking back down the street with Daniel next to him and hands tied behind his back. Jesse and I followed in the wagon not far behind.

When we reached the Sheriff's office, Copley put Daniel in the cell furthest from the entrance. He then called me over to where Daniel was standing behind the bars. "What's this all about anyway? Have you boys been drinking?"

"No Sheriff," I said. "That guy Cartwright robbed us at gunpoint as we were returning home from the war. He saw us resting by a stream and pretended to be friendly. They didn't get much because we didn't have much. We were just poor tired soldiers happy to be alive and wanting to get home. We came into town today to buy supplies for our farm. We weren't looking for any trouble. Cartwright's a criminal, Sheriff and I'm sure you already know that."

"Yeah, he's part of a group here in town that I've been watching. I suspect they've been harassing the Negroes and causing other trouble. I'm keeping an eye on them," Copley said.

"My brother didn't forget that incident Sheriff. When he saw Cartwright today, he couldn't hold back. He just exploded. He was determined to even the score. I know it wasn't right but some things you just can't ignore."

"Well, it's going to cost him a night in jail anyway, disturbing the peace and all that. I'll let him out tomorrow if you promise to stay clear of Cartwright and leave town as soon as you're done with your business."

"We'll pick up supplies tomorrow morning and then we'll be back to get Daniel. You have my word on that, Sheriff."

"Okay, but don't let me catch you or your brother causing any more trouble or you'll be spending more than one night in this jail. You understand?"

"I do Sheriff. I promise you I do."

And, I'd advise you to get your supplies early and get out of town quickly. Those boys may be looking for you. I may not be able to protect you from them."

"Thank you Sheriff. I'll be back early tomorrow morning." I looked over toward Daniel. "Big brother, you take care of yourself. I'll be back in the morning to get you."

Daniel looked back at me and just nodded.

We left the jail and Jesse and I headed toward the Wright House. I was anxious to see Jonathan again but now my news to him would be a little different. I hoped that Daniel would be safe overnight and I was trusting in Sheriff Copley that Daniel would be.

Tomorrow would be another day I thought and I hoped it would go well. I needed to purchase supplies early, pick up Daniel and head home. I also hoped I wouldn't see any sign of Cartwright or his friends.

Chapter 40

Jesse and I got our supplies the next morning, picked up Daniel at the jail and headed for home. It turned out to be an uneventful departure for us, thankfully. We didn't see Cartwright or any of his friends and I was very happy about that. I worried that this wouldn't be the end of the story but it was time for us to get back to farming.

When I arrived home, Cassie and Ella came running out of the house to greet me. I gave my daughter a big hug and Cassie, a big kiss. As always, I had missed them terribly while away but was very happy now to be home. Daniel and Jessie helped me unload my supplies from the wagon and then continued down the road.

"How was your trip?" Cassie asked. "Did you get everything we needed? It looks like you did."

"Yes, I think I remembered everything. The trip was rather quiet too," I said sarcastically with my eyebrow lifted.

"Quiet?" Cassie asked.

"Well, yes, except for the part where Daniel jumped off the wagon and savagely beat a man in Savannah, got arrested and thrown into jail. Other than that, why yes I would say it was quiet."

"Jail, what are you talking about? What happened? I thought you were going into town to buy supplies? Was Daniel drinking?"

"Cassie, you remember me telling you about that fellow Cartwright, who robbed us as we were returning home from the war, don't you? Daniel spotted him as we were riding into town and jumped out of the wagon and went after him. If they hadn't pulled him off he might have killed him too. I don't think I've ever seen Daniel like that. He was insane with anger. I chased after him and tried to break it up. It took several of us a while to get them separated."

"I thought you said Cartwright was a big man. Was Daniel hurt? Is he okay?"

"No, Daniel's fine. But I think he broke Cartwright's jaw and several other parts of his body. He got Cartwright by surprise. I chuckled quietly. It looked like a fox going after an unsuspecting rabbit in the woods, the way it happened so quickly. Daniel spent a night in jail for it. It might've been longer had it not been for a sympathetic sheriff. I don't think he cared for Cartwright any more than we did. We told the sheriff we would pick up our supplies the next morning, get Daniel and then leave town. He was agreeable to that. He warned us to get out of town quickly though and avoid any more trouble with those guys."

"Do you think that's the end of it Micah? Is it over now?"

"I don't know Cassie. I really don't think so. Those fellows are organizing in Savannah and I think there's going to be trouble ahead. I just hope it doesn't find its way to us. How's your father? Have you seen him since we left?"

"He came over to check on us. He's fine. He's waiting on Jesse to return with the supplies. He's ready to start planting."

"That's what I need to do also. I'm going to get started first thing tomorrow morning." With that, I walked into the house wanting to get cleaned up and go to bed early. The planting season was just starting again and I needed all the rest I could get.

"I'll make you a good breakfast tomorrow morning," Cassie said. "We'll get a good early start on the day. We have some long ones ahead of us."

Chapter 41

I'd been working in the fields for several weeks since returning from Savannah, when I heard hollering in the distance. I turned around to see who it was. As he got closer, I recognized that it was Jesse, yelling as he was running toward me.

"Micah, come here. Come here quick. Daniel's been hurt. Come here."

I ran quickly toward him. When I reached him, I grabbed him by the shoulders. "What is it? What's happened?"

"You'd better come quickly. Daniel was beaten up. He needs help. Come quickly."

As I ran with Jesse toward Daniel's place, I tried to get details from him. "How badly is he hurt? Who did it, Jesse?"

"I think he's hurt pretty badly. I saw them riding away. I don't think they saw me."

"Who did you see Jesse? Who did you see riding away? Who was it?"

"It was them."

"Who was it Jesse, who?"

"Those guys we saw in Savannah, Micah. The one who Daniel beat up and some others that were with him that day. You remember him, it was that guy, Cartwright. I saw him riding away with Billy and someone else. I'm not sure who the other one was."

"Cartwright, are you sure?"

"Yeah, it was him alright. I'm sure of it. It was him."

"Let's get to Daniel," I said. "We can deal with them later."

As we came up to Daniel's place, I thought about Aliyah also. "Jesse, did you see Aliyah? Where is she? How is she?"

"No. I didn't see Aliyah. I only saw Daniel. I don't think they harmed her but I'm not sure. I don't know where she is."

I saw Daniel laying on his back and ran over to him. His face was beat up pretty good. He was lying on the ground and moaning. "Daniel, can you hear me. Are you okay?"

He glanced up at me slowly and then looked away.

"Jesse, we need to get him to the doctor. Go get your wagon."

"Okay, I'll be back soon."

I looked back down at Daniel. "Daniel, did you see who did this to you?"

"It was Cartwright and those other weasels," he mumbled. I didn't see them at first. They came up on me quickly while I was cutting a log. I saw them and then I yelled to Aliyah to run. Where is she Micah? Did you see her?"

"Daniel, I don't know where she is now. Jesse said he thought it was them when he came to your house. He hollered for you and it must have scared them away. He doesn't think they saw him. He said he didn't see Aliyah."

"I've got to find Aliyah. Help me get up."

"You're not going anywhere in your condition Daniel. Lay still until we can get you to some help. Jesse's gone to get the wagon."

"I think my arm and some ribs are broken. It hurts when I breathe." He paused then said, "They came up on me so fast, I didn't have time to defend myself. They're nothing but cowards, Micah, every one of them."

"Just lay still Daniel. Don't talk anymore. I don't want you to injure yourself any further."

"Micah, promise me you'll find Aliyah. You've got to promise me you'll find her."

"I'll look for her Daniel. She probably just ran into the woods somewhere. I'll find her Daniel, I promise."

About twenty minutes later, Jesse returned. We loaded Daniel on to the wagon and took him to Dr. Reed.

The doctor examined him. "Micah, he has a broken arm and three broken ribs. He also has a broken nose. He's beat up pretty good."

I thought to myself, we were lucky. If Jesse hadn't come when he did, they would've killed him.

"He needs to stay in bed for a while. Try to keep him quiet and let him rest for a few weeks," Doctor Reed said.

Judging from his injuries, I figured it would take several months for Daniel to heal. The doctor said it would be a while before he could get back to farming. I decided that Daniel should stay at my house and we'd take care of him. I figured he'd be a difficult patient and he'd try to get up and back to farming before he was ready. I was worried more though, about what else might happen. Had we seen the last of Cartwright and his pals? Where had they gone? What would they do next?

We couldn't find Aliyah. She hadn't returned. What had happened to her? Where had she gone? I needed to start looking for her. I knew I needed to find her for Daniel's sake. I also knew that very soon I'd be going back to Savannah.

Chapter 42

"Cassie, I need to find Aliyah. I've got to go back to Savannah. I promised Daniel I'd look for her. He can't do it himself right now. I have to and I need to leave right away."

"Why do you have to go Micah? It might be dangerous. She might be anywhere. Daniel can look for her when he gets better. Maybe she'll just come back on her own in a few days."

"I don't think so, Cassie. You know that we searched the woods all around here and we couldn't find any trace of her. We've asked around and no one has seen her. She may have gone to Savannah or even north toward Charleston. I don't know. But I need to try and find her for Daniel. I need to make sure that she's not hurt; that she's okay. I need to bring her back if she'll come back. Aliyah may be afraid and hiding. She may even be in danger. I have to find out."

"We need you here Micah. Your daughter needs you. I need you. The farm needs you. You can't go Micah. It's much too dangerous. I won't let you go."

"Cassie, please, I must go. I promised Daniel I would try to find her. I'll only be gone a few days. I'll go to Savannah, look around and then come back if I don't find her. I'll be safe, I promise you."

"I'll go with you Micah. I can help you find her."

"No Cassie, you can't go. You need to be here with Ella. Jesse said he'll go with me. We'll go see Jonathan and then the Sheriff. We'll look around Savannah and then come home. I promise you Cassie, I'll only be gone a few days at most."

"What does Daniel say about this?"

"He wants to come with us but he can't. He's in no condition to travel. It'll be weeks before he's up and about. Jesse and I'll be fine. We'll be back soon, I promise. We'll be safe."

"I love you Micah. I don't want you to go but I know you're going anyway. Please take care of yourself. Be very, very careful."

"I will Cassie. We'll be back soon, you'll see."

The next day, Jesse came to the house early in the morning. Cassie made breakfast for us and then we loaded his wagon with some supplies to last us a few days. I said goodbye to Daniel, then Ella and Cassie. I knew our journey to Savannah was risky, though I didn't say so to Cassie. I didn't know what we'd find or what to expect. I appeared optimistic on the outside but I was worried on the inside.

Chapter 43

It took us all day to reach Savannah. We tried to be cautious with Aaron's wagon as we moved along the dusty, rocky, rutted roads on the way to Savannah. The wagon was showing its age now but we knew we needed to keep it around and in working condition. We used it for hauling supplies, moving produce to market and removing trees and other debris while clearing the land. We couldn't afford to buy another one and our two families were depending on this wagon.

"Where're you going friends?" asked a man on a horseback, riding in the opposite direction as we made our way toward the city. "Going to Savannah?"

"Yes we are. We have business there," I replied.

"You should turn around and find business elsewhere. It's not safe there now. There's trouble in the city and it's only going to get worse."

I looked at the man, probably in his mid-forties, with long dark hair, darkly tanned skin and a sadness about him that I hadn't seen since the war. He was probably someone who worked outside for a living, I thought--someone who had been in the city for a while too.

"What's the problem there? I was in Savannah a few months back and it seemed safe. Has it changed?"

"Yes, it's changed. It's not safe anymore. There are bands of whites and Negroes causing trouble around the city. There's no money and no jobs. There are shortages of food, coffee and other necessities. People are struggling to get by. You should turn around and go back from where you came. I'm leaving. I'm not going back. I lost everything I had," he said.

"Well, we can't. I'm very sorry for your loss sir but we're looking for someone and we have to go there. I thank you for your warning but we have no choice. We have to go," I said.

"Well, try to do what you need to do as quickly as possible and don't trust anyone. Watch out for trouble." The stranger looked back to his front and then rode off without saying another word.

In spite of that dire warning, we continued on our journey and soon entered Savannah. I wanted to stop and see Jonathan before we started our search. I knew he would tell us everything we needed to know and his place was convenient for us to stay. It would also be good to see a friendly face again.

On our arrival at the Wright House, we entered and asked for Jonathan. We were tired from our journey and wanted to get a meal and a room for the evening.

"He's out back at the stables but should be in shortly," the Negro male attendant said.

"Okay. We're friends. Please let him know we're waiting outside for him," I said. We walked back out and sat down on a wooden bench next to the walkway leading into the house.

The Wright House had a lovely white porch that surrounded the house on three sides. It had a two-seated swing, hanging from the top of the porch just to the right of where you entered. As I had noted on an earlier visit, gentle breezes were usually blowing through and around the porch, as it was protected from the sun's heat by the large oak trees surrounding the house. The porch, with pots of evenly spaced pink Azalea's sitting on the floor, added to the charm of the house.

As I sat down on the bench, I picked up a newspaper that I saw lying beside it on the ground. A guest must have casually left it sitting there I thought. I browsed the front page story. It talked of the problems the city was facing, trying to keep its neighborhoods clean and accessible. The large numbers of coloreds that had crowded into the city from distressed Plantations and the runaways during the last months of the war was unexpected and a major burden on the city. Also, since the end of the war, Negroes and subsistence farmers from around Georgia and throughout the South had begun migrating to the larger cities mainly looking for work. Savannah was no exception. The over-crowding had created sanitation problems due to garbage and stagnant water in and around the city. Also, the lack of food and clean water was adding to the problems. Disease and sickness were overwhelming the city's ability to deal with it. Articles told of city leaders struggling to find answers as the war had crippled the city and its economy. What had been a vibrant, major shipping port before the war had now been reduced to being a minor economic player nationally.

We waited outside for about fifteen minutes and then Jonathan walked slowly out onto the porch to greet us. He was hobbling along on his hand-crafted crutches. "Hey guys, it's good to see you again. What brings you back to Savannah so soon?"

"We're here on personal business," I said. The colored girl, Aliyah, who lived on our farm for many years, ran away and we're trying to find her. We think she may have come to Savannah."

"Micah, most of the Negroes in town have run away from farms and plantations so why should your slave girl be any different? They're free now. They can do as they please. They have to find their own way. We can't own them anymore Micah. She's no longer your property. She's free to go where she pleases and you can't do anything about it. As you've probably noticed, I have several former slaves working here for me."

"You don't understand Jonathan, Aliyah and Daniel were very close. The three men we had the run-in with the last time we were here, came out to Daniel's place and beat him up pretty badly. Aliyah ran away in fear of her life. She wasn't looking to leave. She ran away because she had to—she was scared. There's no telling what they would've done to her. We've looked all around the farm and surrounding areas and we haven't been able to find her anywhere. I hope she's safe somewhere but I don't know where. We want to try and find her and we think she may have come here."

"Wow. That's going to be very tough Micah. You're not going to get much help from the white folks around here and probably none at all from the coloreds. They're looking to protect their people from the whites; especially their women. They won't trust you. It'll be very dangerous for you."

"Jonathan, I have to try. I need to find out what's happened to her. I promised Daniel."

"How is Daniel? Was he hurt badly? Will he be okay?"

"He has some broken bones and ribs. The doctor says he'll get better but it's going to take some time until he's up and about. He's staying at my place for now while he improves. Cassie's looking after him."

"What about those three guys you were talking about? What if you run into them again while you're here in Savannah? I don't think they're going to treat you any different than they treated Daniel. Do they know that you know it was them?"

"You mean Cartwright and the others? They don't know that we're looking for them. That's to our advantage. Jesse saw them ride away from Daniel's place but he doesn't think they saw him. We're going to look for Aliyah first, and then we'll figure out what to do about them later. I'm planning on visiting the Sheriff to let him know what's happened. Maybe he can help us. I sure hope so. Can we stay here for a couple of days? Do you have room for us Jonathan?"

"It's not a problem. You're always welcome here and I have a room open. If I didn't have one, I would find room somewhere even if you had to sleep in the stable. You can take your horse and wagon around back. I'll take good care of them while you're here."

"Thank you Jonathan. You've always been very helpful. I'm grateful," I said.

As we started to walk around to the back of the house, I could see that Jonathan had a concerned look on his face. "Be very careful Micah. It's not safe here now." He paused, "Let me know if you need anything while you're here. I'll help you if I can."

"Thanks again Jonathan. That's very generous of you. I know we can count on your help if we need it."

Chapter 44

We got up the next morning, had a nice breakfast and headed out in the direction of the Sheriff's office. It was a sunny, pretty morning but it started to get warm early.

"I hope the Sheriff can help us Jesse. I want to find out what he knows about the coloreds' who've come into Savannah. I want to know if he's seen or even knows where they're going when they first come into town. Also, I want to tell him about Cartwright and the others and what they did to Daniel. He'll want to know about that. Hopefully, he'll be willing to help us."

"He seemed like a fair man to me Micah. He could have been a lot tougher on Daniel than he was. Maybe he will help us."

We arrived at the Sheriff's office at around nine o'clock. As I walked in to his office, I looked around slowly. It looked a little different than before. It seemed liked there were less chairs and tables and much more clutter. There were magazines and newspapers in several piles and what looked like old clothes in others. I remembered that Sheriff Copley liked a clean jail. The area seemed strangely different now.

After we had been there for a few moments, a rough looking character walked out from the back room where the cells were located and asked, "Who you boys looking for?" The man had long hair, a chiseled face and appeared to be chewing tobacco. I also noticed that he had a slight limp.

"We're looking for Sheriff Copley," I replied. "Is he here?"

He stared at me for a moment or two and then said, "No he's not here." He then turned his head slowly to his left side and spit a dark substance on to the floor. He then looked back at me.

"Do you know when he'll be back?" I asked.

"He's not coming back," the man replied. "He's gone. He left town a few weeks back and no one has seen him. Nobody knows what happened to him. He just up and left."

I looked at Jesse curiously as my heart was slowly sinking. "When did you say he left town?" I asked, with a questioning tone to my voice.

"A few weeks ago," the man replied. "You're asking a lot of questions too. What do you want? Why are you here?"

"I was just looking for the Sheriff. We wanted to talk with him. We had things to discuss with him."

"Well, the new Sheriff should be back soon. He's making his rounds. I'll tell him you were here. What are your names anyway?" he asked.

"Tell him Micah and Jesse came by to see him. We want to talk with him when he has time. What's the new Sheriff's name?"

"We call him Sheriff Billy. Billy Dale's his full name," he replied. "He's been the Sheriff now for a week. He's giving this town some real law and order."

I turned and looked at Jesse incredibly and paused. "How could this be?" I mumbled quietly.

"What'd you say?" the man asked, giving me a hard look.

"Nothing, I didn't say anything. Tell Sheriff Billy we're in town and just dropped by to say hello. He knows us. I served in the war with him. We'll be back later this week.   "We're   in   town   for   a   few   days   buying   supplies."

"Suit yourself," the man replied, as we turned and walked out the door. "Suit yourself."

I hadn't expected Sheriff Copley to be gone. I wondered what had happened to him and why he'd leave town so soon. Was he run out of town, I wondered? Was he even still alive? I knew my trip to Savannah would be difficult but now it had become even more so.

Chapter 45

"This can't be," Jesse said. "Why would Sheriff Copley just up and leave town? It doesn't make sense Micah. Something is seriously wrong in this town. Maybe we should just leave and come back when things cool down a little around here."

"We can't do that Jesse. I promised Daniel. We owe it to Aliyah to try and find her regardless of the risks. She may be in trouble and need our help."

"It just doesn't seem safe here, Micah. What if Aliyah isn't here? What if we run into that Billy Dale and his friends again?"

"He doesn't know that we know it was him and Cartwright that beat up Daniel. We need to remain quiet about that until the time is right. They mustn't find out."

"What about Aliyah? Maybe she didn't even come here. Maybe she headed to the Carolina's like you said. It'll be like looking for a needle in a haystack. Actually, I think our chances would be better at finding a needle because no one would be trying to stop us. Before it's over, we may have the coloreds and Billy Dale looking for us. That won't be pleasant Micah."

"Look Jesse. I'm asking too much for you to stay here with me. Why don't you take the wagon and head back to the farm? There's no sense in you risking harm here. I'll look around for a few days and if I can't find her, I'll come home. I won't do anything stupid."

"You're not going to be alone here either, Micah. I'm staying with you. I promised Cassie I would look out for you and I'm not going anywhere. I just want us to do everything we can to be safe. We both have families at home waiting and depending on us."

"I know Jesse. I promise we won't take any unnecessary risks while we're here."

The rest of our day was spent down by the river and docks, looking around but without much luck. We saw hundreds of Negro dockworkers loading cotton on to ships but there was no sign of Aliyah. I knew that tomorrow we would have to go into the colored areas of town and look around down there. That was where we would have our best chance of finding Aliyah if she was in fact, in Savannah.

"Let's head back to Jonathan's now and get a good night's rest Jesse. We've done all we can do today. We'll continue our search tomorrow."

We headed back to the Wright House that evening knowing that the task ahead of us was a formidable one. Could we even find Aliyah? I knew our odds were slim. Would we be looking in the right areas of town? Was she even in Savannah? Maybe she had fled to the Carolinas. We had a lot of questions and very few answers. Those questions can wait until tomorrow, I thought to myself. For tonight, I was hoping for a good night's rest.

Chapter 46

We got up the next morning and went downstairs for breakfast. The delicious smell of ham and bacon cooking in the kitchen stirred our senses. Jesse and I walked into the dining room and sat down around a long mahogany table that seated twelve. Jesse and I sat at one end and a few moments later, others came in and joined us.

"Good morning. I'm John Wells and this is my wife Sally. We're down from Boston."

"It's nice to meet you. I'm Micah and this is Jesse. We're here on personal business. What brings you to Savannah?"

"We're going to be teaching coloreds in a local schoolhouse within the city. We understand there are a lot of them here and we're looking to give them a little schooling. We've come south to help them learn to read and write. You know, teach them the three R's."

"What kind of business are you in?" Sally asked.

"We're farmers and we're in town to purchase supplies. We live about fifty miles southwest of here. Our farms and families are there," I said.

"Interesting," said John. "What do you farm?"

"We grow cotton, vegetables and we have some animals--chickens, pigs and cows. We have less now than we had before the war but we're getting by okay. Times are tough down here now and we're thankful for what we do have."

"We saw that," said Sally. "I mean, as we traveled south by train, we saw the destruction from the war and the desperation of the people along the route. Many buildings and factories were burned or torn down even in the smaller towns. In villages along the way, we saw people wearing old and worn clothing. Many didn't even have shoes. Things are quite different here than up North. Business is growing back there and cities are alive and active. People seem to be more happy and content with their lives too than here. War sure has strange and cruel consequences doesn't it?"

"Please understand, we don't mean to insult you," John said. "We were just shocked by the devastation that we've seen. We didn't expect it to be this bad."

"The war has caused tremendous suffering in the South. We haven't adjusted yet to the new reality. It'll probably take months, even years, I suppose. But we have other issues down here now and those are causing problems for us too. Gangs of whites have formed to harass and terrorize the Negroes that have come into the city. They want to return things to like they were before the war. They don't see the Negroes as their equals. I hope you'll be very careful while you're here," I said.

"I don't think we're under any illusions about how bad things are but there is much good to be done and we hope to get started soon," said John. "We're religious people and the good lord is surely watching out for us in this worthy cause."

"Just the same, keep an eye on your back. There are some bad people in this town and you'd better beware," Jesse said.

"We thank you for your words of caution. Well, I see breakfast is coming and we'd better eat it while it's hot," said John, as two colored female servers brought food to the table.

A few minutes later Johnathan came in to the dining room. "I see you've already met," said Jonathan, walking in slowly on crutches and sitting down to have breakfast with us. He had been working in the kitchen when we first sat down. "Hope this morning's breakfast is to your liking," he said with a broad smile on his face.

"Its fine, Jonathan. I especially like these fig preserves. Do you make them yourself?" I asked.

"No, I buy them locally. I've always had a sweet tooth and I love fig preserves. I always assume that my guests will too."

"I enjoyed them also. We don't see these back in Boston unless they've come from somewhere else. The weather's too cold for Fig trees to grow there," said John. He then looked at me. "What are you fellows doing today?"

"Jesse and I are going down to the colored Baptist Church to look around. Maybe talk to the preacher there. We want to see if we can get some information," I said.

"It's none of my business but why are you going there, Micah? Do you buy supplies from them?" asked John.

"No, we're looking for a girl that used to live on our farm. There was an incident recently and she ran away. We hope to find her if she's here in Savannah," I said.

"I don't understand," said John. "Oh, I'm sorry, I don't mean to pry but what kind of incident could've occurred that would cause a girl to run away from her farm?"

"It's okay to ask." I paused and looked around. "She's a colored girl, who worked on our farm and ran away when some evil men came to our farm looking for trouble. They beat up my brother Daniel and Aliyah ran away. Aliyah's the girl. We want to find her if we can," I said.

John looked at me quizzically and then said, "You're not slave catchers are you?"

"No John, we're not slave catchers, I promise you that. Aliyah was raised as one of our family and we want to find her to see that she's okay. We care for her. We would never harm her," I said.

"Be careful down there Micah. The coloreds are not very fond of white folks. They'll be very cautious and probably silent too. There may also be gangs of coloreds down there looking to cause trouble just like the whites are doing. Be very careful, please," Jonathan said.

"We will Jonathan." I then looked at Jesse and said, "I think we need to get going." I then turned back to John and Sally, "It's been a pleasure spending time with you this morning. I look forward to seeing you again. Good luck with your schooling. I hope you're successful."

"Thank you Micah. Please be cautious today," said John.

"We will," I replied.

It was very nice meeting John and Sally at breakfast. My impression of them was that they were good people with big hearts. Their plan to teach the coloreds in Savannah was surely necessary but it was a road strewn with danger. The coloreds had come to town in large numbers, many without education or skills and would need a lot of help if they were ever going to be able to take care of themselves. But Jesse and I were on a mission too and it was now time for us to get on with it.

Chapter 47

We started down Montgomery Street looking for the colored Baptist church. Jonathan had said that it was one of the original churches in the area. Finished just prior to the civil war, its history dated back to the late 1700's. Jonathan mentioned a Reverend Thomas who he had met a few months earlier. He said the Reverend had been at the church for several years and he might be able to provide information to us about runaways coming in to town. He said that Thomas would be familiar with the coloreds' who had followed Sherman into Savannah and the arrivals since then but whether or not he would share that information with us would be the question. For now, at least, it was our best option.

"Jesse, I'm hoping Reverend Thomas will help us. He knows the Negro community and may have had contact with Aliyah or know of someone who has."

"I don't know. I think it's a long shot Micah. As Jonathan said, they don't trust whites down there. I just hope they're peaceful toward us. I don't want any trouble."

"Well, we'll see Jesse. Hopefully someone can give us information that will lead us to her."

As we got closer to Franklin Square we could see the church in the distance. It had an impressive steeple that reached upward into the sky. On this day, it provided a beautiful silhouette against a broad blue background. I could also see the large windows on the side of the brick building. I was in awe as I looked at it. Jonathan told me it had been built by slaves. Its bricks, made of sand and clay rocks found by the river, had been made by slaves living and working on plantations, laboring in the evenings to complete it. I was anxious to go inside and look around.

As we got closer to the church, I noticed groups of coloreds that were standing around in front of it as we moved slowly along in our wagon. Those who were standing near the corner of the building by the road, watched us suspiciously as we pulled up and climbed down from the wagon.

"I'm looking for Reverend Thomas," I said to the group standing near the entrance to the church. There were an equal number of men and women standing there together. "Do you know where I might find him?"

Without saying a word, one of the young colored males turned slowly and pointed to the entrance to the church. I saw another male nod in agreement.

"Thank you," I said, as we walked slowly toward the front of the building. There were stairways on both sides leading up to the entrance to the sanctuary.

We pushed open the large wooden doors and looked inside. The elevated pulpit was to our front with large, glass windows inside on both sides of the building. Wooden pews were neatly organized on a wooden floor. I looked up and saw a balcony which I assumed had seating surrounding the inside of the sanctuary. I had never seen anything like this before and I was struck by its modest beauty.

As we continued to gaze around the interior, I noticed from the corner of my eye a large, colored man coming toward me.

"You fellows looking for me," he said in a low but powerful voice. "I'm Reverend Thomas. What can I do for you?" A quick glimpse of Reverend Thomas confirmed that he was a large man. I estimated him at about six-foot two and well over two hundred pounds. He was middle-aged, with partially graying hair. He looked like a man who had labored most of his life and had a rugged, sturdy appearance.

I held out my hand to him and he slowly grabbed it and gave it a firm shake. "Reverend Thomas, my name is Micah and this is my friend Jesse. We're farmers. We live about fifty miles southwest of here. A girl left our farm a few weeks ago and we believe she may have come to Savannah."

"Is she a colored girl?" he asked.

"Yes, Reverend, she is. Her name is Aliyah and she grew up on our farm. She's lived her whole life there. We came to find her, to see how she's doing. We mean her no harm, Reverend. We're here to help her if she needs it. That's all we want. Can you help us?"

He looked slowly, first at me then at Jesse. He took a moment or two before he questioned, "Are you slave catchers? That's over now. The war is done. There'll be no more of that," he said firmly.

"No, Reverend, I swear we're not. Aliyah was free to leave of her own free will. We know that. We're only trying to find Aliyah to see if she needs help. We want to make sure she's not in danger. Can you help us? Have you seen her?" I asked.

"No, I haven't seen her and I don't believe I would tell you if I had. If she's here, then she's safe here. Safe from your kind," he said.

I looked over at Jesse, paused for a moment then muttered, "Let's go. It seems we're not going to get much help here." As we walked away slowly, I looked back at the Reverend and said, "We only want to help her."

I was not only upset but hurt. I had hoped that Reverend Thomas would help us. I didn't expect to be rejected like that; my intentions to be so misunderstood. The Reverend didn't seem to be hateful toward us but he didn't seem too friendly either.

"Jesse, I want to ride a little further down the road and see what we can find. I doubt that the Reverend knows everyone who's come into town. Maybe we'll get lucky on our own."

"Okay, but we need to be careful," he said.

We got into the wagon and pulled away from the church. I didn't know where we would go now but I knew that I had to continue looking for Aliyah just a little bit longer.

Chapter 48

We departed the church knowing we had several hours of daylight left to continue our search. The sun would be dropping to the horizon soon on this warm early summer day. I was hoping for at least some information about Aliyah before we had to head back. So far we didn't have much. I was worried about being in this area too long and especially during the hours of darkness.

"Jesse, let's go down this road a ways and see what we find," I said. As we traveled along the road, parallel with the river, the area appeared increasingly depressed. I saw garbage on both sides of the road and rats playing between the piles. The stench was overwhelming. Pools of stagnant water lay everywhere, serving the insect and vermin populations. I occasionally covered my nose with my hand to block the odors that were challenging my sense of smell.

"Micah, I don't know about this area. It doesn't look safe to me. Maybe we should turn around and come back tomorrow morning."

"We will Jesse. I just want to look a little further. Let's go a few more blocks and then we'll turn around."

We were about four blocks from the church when I saw a group of young colored men standing on the corner as we approached. As our wagon got closer to the corner, several of them moved out in front of our wagon. They moved to the middle of the road blocking our path forward.

"Where're you going, white boys?" one of them asked, in a barely audible tone. The man speaking, apparently their leader was tall and thin, a darker black skinned fellow with scars showing on his arms and face. His eyes were steely and penetrating.

He looked to be in his early twenties but someone who had experienced great pain and suffering in a short lifetime. I'd seen that same sterile look from soldiers who were badly fatigued and beaten after a battle lost.

"We're looking for someone," I replied.

"Well, you're not going to be looking down here," he said. As he spoke, I noticed that the others with him had surrounded our wagon.

"Who're you looking for anyway?" another asked. I paused for a moment, trying to come up with a non-offensive reply.

"A girl," Jesse said. "Her name is Aliyah. We want to talk with her. We believe she may be here."

I shuttered at Jesse's reply. I was concerned now where this conversation would go.

"Well, she's not here," their leader said. "You'd better turn that wagon around and get out of here while you still can."

I looked at Jesse and then said, "Turn the wagon around. Let's go."

As the wagon slowly turned, I felt a sudden jolt. I looked toward Jesse and saw that he had been pulled to the ground. A moment later, I too was yanked hard to the ground. I was being punched and kicked by several attackers as I writhed in pain. I heard Jesse screaming. I thought to myself--this is the end, we're not going to get away. The punching and kicking continued for what seemed like forever and then I heard it--a loud bellowing voice. It seemed that an angel had now interceded.

"Stop it! Get off of them. Let them go now!"

I looked up with swollen and partially closed eyes and saw Reverend Thomas. Where had he come from? I could not believe what was happening.

"I said let them go," bellowed Thomas again, grabbing one of the fellows holding Jesse and throwing him to the ground. He then looked at us and with a commanding voice said, "Get back in the wagon."

I got up slowly and crawled back into the wagon. My body was aching in too many places to count. Jesse also got up. I looked at Jesse, happy to see that he too was still alive. I could see that he was bleeding from his head and his mouth. He had bruises on his arms and held his wrist as if it were broken. I took a deep breath as my heart continued to pound rapidly. I looked down. I was dripping blood. My lip was split open. My ribs ached from several hard kicks. I was hurting but glad to be alive.

We headed back to the church. Reverend Thomas had jumped onto the back of the wagon riding with us.

"Pull over by the front," Thomas said, as he pointed toward the entrance to the church. "We'll patch you boys up before you head home."

Jesse pulled the wagon up close to the stairs at the front of the church. We got down slowly from the wagon. I couldn't move any faster. I was fortunate that I could still walk. I followed Reverend Thomas into the sanctuary. After walking through the large front doors we turned into the room that was on the left.

"Come in here," Thomas directed. We walked in and sat down on chairs he had pushed toward us. "Millie, go get some rags and water," he said, to a small colored girl who had come in to see what the commotion was all about.

We had been there for about an hour or so, getting cleaned up, when the Reverend said to us, "You boys had better stay here tonight. I don't want you going outside in your condition. You shouldn't be on the road at this hour anyway. You can eat here tomorrow morning and then leave. I suggest you stay away from this area in the future. I don't think I need to tell you but you're not safe, nor welcome around here."

"Thank you Reverend. You saved us for sure. Thank you for being there today," I said.

"You were very foolish to go down there. You're lucky to be alive."

"I know. Thank you again Reverend."

Millie brought us a couple of blankets and pointed to the floor. "You can sleep here tonight. I'll bring you some food in the morning."

"Thank you," I said. "We'll be fine here."

After the reverend and Millie had walked away, I turned and looked at Jesse. "Are you okay? Your face is red and swollen and you have bruises all over your body. I'm so sorry Jesse. I'm sorry that I got you involved in all of this. This was not your problem."

"It could have been much worse Micah. We could've been killed. We're lucky we weren't. It's time for us to go home."

"I know," I said.

With that, we laid down on the hard floor to rest for the evening. I was still in a lot of pain and probably would be for several days. I was thankful however, to still be breathing. I was also grateful that Jesse was still alive, since I had gotten him into this awful mess in the first place. Sadly, I knew we weren't any closer to finding Aliyah. Our time spent and the journey to this place had been fruitless. It was time to go home now. We would begin our journey in the morning.

Chapter 49

Jesse and I woke up the next morning to the smell of fresh coffee and warm biscuits. "You boys hungry?" Millie asked.

"We sure are and those biscuits smell great," I replied, still lying flat on my back. I looked up at Millie who was carrying a plate stacked with warm biscuits. I could see heat rising from the plate and the pleasant aroma was filling the room. It reminded me of the fresh biscuits Cassie made for me back home.

As I began to get up, I realized that I had moved too quickly. My body was screaming in pain from the beating I had taken the day before--the consequences of foolishly going too far into an unknown and dangerous area. My whole body was aching. I heard Jesse groan as he emerged from a deep sleep.

"I made fresh coffee if you boys would like some," Millie said.

"I was a soldier Millie. You can be sure I enjoy a cup of coffee in the morning. I think Jesse would too," I said, looking at him—that is, if he can get up. He doesn't look too good this morning.

"I'll be okay in a moment. I don't want to break any more bones trying to get up. Yes mam, I'd love a cup," Jesse replied.

"It's funny," I said, "during the war, because of the Union blockade, it became hard for us to get coffee. Now it's always a surprise to me and seems like such a luxury when it's offered. I'll probably never say "no" again to a cup of coffee when it's offered."

I reached over to the plate that Millie had put on the small brown table next to us and grabbed two of the steaming biscuits. I took one bite, looked up at Millie and gave her my approval with a big smile. She seemed pleased. "These are wonderful Millie. We're very grateful. We'll just finish our coffee and then be on our way back home. Is Reverend Thomas here this morning?"

"He's doing some work out back. I'll see if I can get him to come in," Millie said and walked from the room.

"Jesse, let's finish our coffee and head out. Before we go though, I want to see the Reverend and thank him again for helping us yesterday and for the kindness this morning. Then, we need to get going. I'm sure Ella and Cassie are anxious to see me and your father will be looking for you."

"Okay, you're right. We need to thank him again for saving our lives yesterday. He didn't have to do that. He risked his own life by jumping in there the way he did."

I looked back toward Jesse to acknowledge his thought when I heard a soft familiar voice coming from behind us.

"Micah, is it you?"

It had been a while since I had heard that sweet voice. I looked back and saw that it was Aliyah. "Aliyah," I blurted out and jumped up quickly to give her a big hug. "Aliyah, are you okay? We were so worried about you. We didn't know where you were or if you were hurt. It's so good to see you again." Tears of joy were flowing down both of our cheeks. "We've missed you so much."

"Hi Aliyah," Jesse said as he walked over to her and gave her a warm embrace. "We're so happy that we've found you."

"I've been here," Aliyah said, "working at the church with Reverend Thomas, helping the new arrivals get settled. It's a busy job and more and more come every day. It's so hard for us to keep up. They need so much and they just keep coming."

"After that night at Daniel's farm we didn't know what had happened to you. We looked everywhere. I thought there might be a chance that you came here, to Savannah," I said.

"How is Daniel? Is he alive? Is he okay? Those men that came were evil. It was getting dark. They surprised us while we were working outside. Daniel told me to run and I did. I hid in the woods for a while and then I left. I didn't stop again until I came here. I didn't know what had happened to Daniel. Reverend Thomas helped me when I arrived here. He gave me food and a place to stay. He saved me," Aliyah said.

"They beat up Daniel pretty badly that night but luckily, Jesse came and surprised them before they could hurt him anymore. They rode off when they heard Jesse calling out for him. Daniel asked me to try and find you. He's very worried about you. He wants you to come back to him. Will you come back with us, Aliyah?" I asked.

"I can't Micah. I love Daniel but I can't. It won't work. There are too many things working against us. I want to see him again but I can't go back. I need to stay here," Aliyah said. "I'm needed here."

"Aliyah, he loves you. He's building the farm for you. I don't think he wants to live without you. You have to go to him. Please, will you come back with us?"

"I can't Micah. It has to be over now. I'm sorry."

"Will you please come back with us to see him? I don't think he'll believe me if I tell him. He has to hear it from you, Aliyah."

"Micah, I can't go back. Please tell him I'll always love him but it just wouldn't work. Good bye Micah," Aliyah said, with tears running down her cheeks.

She turned slowly and began to walk away. Everything in my body was telling me to try and stop her--to bring her back to Daniel. Things will work out I thought, if only I can persuade her. As she slowly walked out the door, I looked at Jesse. He could see and feel my disappointment, my sadness. I knew deep down that Aliyah was right. It had to be over.

Jesse put his arm on my shoulder and looked at me. "Micah let's go home. We're done here. We've done all we can do."

I looked at him, nodded and said "okay."

We left the church and walked outside toward the wagon. I didn't even remember to say goodbye to the Reverend. I looked back at the church one last time, and then said to Jesse, "Let's go home."

Chapter 50

We departed Savannah that morning having mixed emotions. On the one hand, we had found Aliyah and she was safe and doing well--we were very happy about that. But we were unable to convince her to come home with us. That was unfortunate. Maybe it was better for her to stay in Savannah with her own people, I thought. She seemed to be doing okay and was content. They were taking good care of her. She was doing important work. But I knew that Daniel would not take the news very well. I wondered if he would even believe me when I told him of my conversation with Aliyah. His reaction might even be anger towards me for failing in my mission. I knew though, that we had done all that we could in Savannah and I was tired and ready to go home.

"Hey Micah, wait a minute," I heard someone holler from behind us. "I heard you wanted to see me."

I turned back to look at who was calling but I had already recognized that voice. It was Billy Dale. "Hi Billy, we're just leaving town. I stopped by to pay my regards to Sheriff Copley but they said he was gone. I understand you're the new Sheriff now? We just came into town to get some supplies and find out what the market's paying for cotton. We've been here a few days now so it's time for us to leave."

"Yeah, too bad about Sheriff Copley. They found him dead the other night in the river. He must have gotten drunk and fell in and drowned. They made me temporary sheriff to fill in until they can replace him. I want this job real bad. This town needs me."

I looked at Jesse in disbelief, then back at Billy. "I'm sorry to hear of Sheriff Copley. He was a good man. Well, good luck Billy. There's a lot of work to do here and that's for sure."

"What happened to you guys anyway? You look like you got into a brawl with a bear."

"We got into a little skirmish outside a tavern. A fellow there argued we should have continued the war and I argued against it. It seems people here still have strong feelings about the war."

"Well, it looks to me like you boys lost the argument. Better take care of those wounds when you get home."

"We will. It'll take a few weeks though to heal properly," I said.

"How's Daniel, Micah? I see he didn't come with you. I heard that he had gotten injured or something. Is he okay?"

I saw from the corner of my eye the surprised look Jesse had on his face but I didn't want to react to that, at least not in front of Billy. "He's getting better I believe. Some drifters came through our area one evening and beat him up pretty good. He didn't get a look at them because it was dark and Jesse surprised them-- scared them off. He said it must have been some renegade soldiers wandering the area looking for things to steal. Seems like there are plenty of those type folks are out there these days. I'm sure you have your hands full with drifters in town."

"Yeah, that's true. Well, if I hear of anything Micah, I'll let you know. We're having quite a time of it here just keeping these coloreds in order. They just keep coming into town. There's not much here for them either. Many of them left plantations to come here. They're a big problem for us and we're going to have to deal with it one way or another. Oh, by the way, what happened to that little colored girl that was on your farm? Is she still there?"

"No, she ran away the night those drifters beat up Daniel. I suppose she headed toward South Carolina. I think she has family up there, in the Charleston area. We haven't seen her since. She was a hard worker. We hated to see her go," I said.

"Well, you take care, Micah. Maybe I'll come out and visit you one of these days. I want to see Daniel also--you know, see how he's doing, if he'll see me. He was a good soldier. I have a lot of respect for him."

"It's going to be a while before he's up and about. He got beat up pretty good. It'll probably be a few more months I suppose. He's anxious to get back to farming but he's not physically able to yet. The doctor told him not to rush it."

"Okay, you take care," Billy said and walked away in the opposite direction.

"Micah, you lied to him. You told him we didn't know who beat up Daniel. We know who it was. It was him and those snakes he has for friends."

"I know Jesse. But I didn't want him to know that we knew just yet. I want him to go on believing that we don't know who it was. I wanted to buy some time, that's all. We can deal with them later."

"What about Aliyah, Micah. You told him she has family in Charleston and was probably headed there. I thought she was staying in Savannah. Was that true?"

"No, it's not true. But, Aliyah will be much safer if Billy doesn't know she's here in Savannah. I didn't want to tell him anything that he didn't need to know."

"Yeah, I suppose that was smart. I hope he doesn't run into her one day by some coincidence. Being the Sheriff, I'm sure he gets around a lot. I imagine he's causing plenty of trouble for the darkies too."

"Jesse, let's go. I'm anxious to get home."

Chapter 51

It was great to be home and see Ella and Cassie again. I was surprised by how much Ella seemed to have grown in just a short amount of time. I guess I had been consumed with other thoughts the last few weeks.

"Where did you get all of those cuts and bruises Micah?

"We made a wrong turn while in Savannah. We ran into some folks who didn't want us there."

"Micah, I told you it wasn't safe. You could have been killed. Are you okay?"

"Yes. I'll be fine. We tried to be careful, just as I'd promised. Unfortunately, we went into an area that we should've avoided. There were some kind people though, who helped us."

"We really missed you. Ella needs her father and I need you. Ella's very helpful when you're not here. She follows me around and wants to do what I'm doing. Ella asks for you the whole time you're gone. She kept asking when you'd be back. You need to stay home now. You're safe here."

"I missed you both very much. We were away longer than I expected. I know we have a lot of work to do. I'm ready to get started. But, I need to talk with Daniel. Do you know where he is? Did he go back to his place?"

"He left yesterday. He said he needed to get home and see what needed to be done. I don't think he's coming back. He took all of his things with him," Cassie said.

"I'm going over tomorrow morning to talk with him. I need to tell him about my visit to Savannah."

"What did you find? Did you see Aliyah?"

I looked at her carefully, slowly and then said, "Yes, I did. She's fine but she won't be coming back here. She's staying in Savannah. I think that's the best place for her too. They'll look out for her there. She'll be safe."

"Who'll look out for her? Is she staying with someone?" Cassie asked.

"She's staying at the colored Baptist Church in Savannah. They're helping the new arrivals when they come into town. She seems contented and they seem to like her there. I think she'll be fine," I said.

"But what will Daniel say to that?"

"I don't think he'll be too happy to hear what I have to say. But I have to tell him. I have to tell him that I saw Aliyah and talked with her."

I got up the next morning and headed over to Daniel's place. I hadn't been there in several weeks so I didn't know what the place would look like or what to expect.

"Daniel, are you here?" I called out.

"I'm around back," I heard, echoing through the trees. "Come around back."

"Daniel, you're up and about. I didn't expect that."

"I couldn't stay indoors any longer. I was getting sores on my ass and back. I have things to do. I needed to get back. So what did you find out in Savannah? Did you find Aliyah?"

"Yes. I saw Aliyah. She's working at a Baptist Church in Savannah. It's a church for the coloreds. She's happy there and they're good to her." I paused for a moment, considering my next comment. "She's not coming back Daniel. They need her there."

He looked at me with tensing eyes and I sensed our friendly conversation was starting to fade. "What do you mean, she's not coming back? I want her back here Micah. She'll be safe here with me. I'll take care of her. She's got to come back."

"They're good to her Daniel. They'll look after her. Savannah has become a destination for many of the coloreds leaving plantations. She's helping the church take care of those newly arrived. She's needed there and she feels that she's wanted. She seems happy."

"She's wanted back here too," he said abruptly. Her home is here. I've got to go to Savannah and bring her back. She'll come back with me. I know she will. I have to see her."

"Daniel. She's free now. The war's over. She doesn't have to come back here. She can go wherever she wants. I don't think it's safe for her being back here now anyway."

"I don't give a damn what you think Micah. She belongs here. She belongs here with me. I want her here. I'll go to Savannah and bring her back with me."

"I saw Billy Dale in town. He's the Sheriff now and they're making it tough on the coloreds. Aliyah is safe though. She's with her own people."

"I'm her people. It's about time I pay a visit to Savannah and to Billy. I owe him and his friends. Look what they did to me. They won't get away with it, I promise you. I'll kill them if I see them."

"He's the law now Daniel. It would be very dangerous for you to go there. They don't know that we know that it was them who did this to you. I told Billy it was drifters. But it's still not safe for you to go there."

"You're right. It's not safe. It's going to be a very dangerous place for Billy when I find him and his friends. I have to find Aliyah too. She'll come back with me. I know she will."

I left Daniel's place that day thinking there would be more trouble ahead. I knew it was just a matter of time until the situation grew worse. I hoped to avoid it but I wasn't confident I could do so. It was like seeing a deadly fire approaching in the distance but having nowhere to run.

Chapter 52

Several days later, I was out in the fields clearing trees from an area that I wanted to plant in the spring. It was hot and humid and I was ready for a break. I paused to wipe my brow and take a drink of water. My shirt was drenched in perspiration and specks of dirt littered my face, hands and arms.

"Micah, Micah, come quickly," I heard Cassie yell from the edge of the field. She was walking quickly toward me.

I wondered what could've happened for her to be as alarmed as that. Had something happened to Ella? Did the animals get loose? Was there a fire in the barn? What could it be I wondered?

"Cassie, what is it? What's happened?"

"Daniel came to the house. He took your gun. He looked at me and said it was time he went to Savannah and take care of some business. Then he quickly turned and walked out the door. He didn't say anything else. He had a grave look on his face Micah. I haven't seen him like that before."

"This isn't good Cassie. I need to find him and stop him before he does something he'll regret later. I need to go now."

"You can't Micah. It's too dangerous there. Please don't go back to Savannah. You could be killed. You've been there several times already. You can't go again. You've done all you can do. I forbid you to go."

"I have to find Daniel. There's no telling what he'll do. I need to try and stop him."

"Stop him from what Micah? You can't stop him. He's going to do what he's going to do. You can't go there again Micah, it's not safe."

"I'm sorry Cassie. He's my brother. I have to go. I don't have any time to waste. I need to leave now and try to find him."

With that, I quickly turned and headed back to the house leaving Cassie behind. I packed a few things, gave Ella and Cassie hugs and then started on my way. I didn't have Jesse's wagon, so the trip would take longer this time but I was hoping to hitch a ride along the way.

I entered the city a day later and even though it was early in the morning, I decided to stop and see Jonathan first. I wanted to ask him if he'd seen Daniel or had any news about what might be happening in town.

Entering the Wright House, I didn't see anyone so I asked loudly, "Is Jonathan here?"

There was a few seconds of silence and then I heard Jonathan coming up the hallway, "I'm here. I'm slow but I'm coming. Breakfast should be ready soon." He then saw me and said, "Micah, what are you doing here? I thought you'd gone home."

"Jonathan, I need to talk with you."

"Okay Micah, let's go outside. We can talk there."

We walked through the front porch and took a seat on the wrought iron bench next to the walkway. It was very comfortable with the early morning breeze blowing gently under the huge Oak trees.

"Could you bring us some tea Lettie?" Jonathan asked a colored lady who was cleaning the rocking chairs on the front porch. "Lettie's a wonderful worker. She's been with our family since before the war and continues to work for us--but now I have to pay her for her work. Interesting how things have changed, isn't it Micah?"

"Yes. Things have changed in many ways--mostly for the worst unfortunately."

"What brings you back to town so quickly, Micah? You did leave didn't you?"

"Yes, I did. I'm looking for Daniel. Have you seen him?"

"No, I haven't. I thought you said he was injured. What's up? Is something wrong?"

"I hope not but I need to find him. He's come to town and I'm concerned there might be trouble. Those guys that beat him up, well, they're here in Savannah. Daniel may be looking for them. I need to find him before something bad happens."

"What do you think he'd do?"

"To tell you the truth Jonathan, I don't know what he'd do. He's angry and he's carrying around a hunger for revenge. That's why I need to find him before he finds them."

"Where will you look Micah?"

"I'm going down to the colored Baptist Church. He might be there."

"Why would he be there?"

"He's probably looking for Aliyah. You remember I mentioned the colored girl who lived on our farm? I don't recall telling you before but he and Aliyah were very close. He wants to take her back with him to the farm. He believes that she's in Savannah and that she will go back with him."

"Are you serious? Wow. That's something. If he's gone down there it could be dangerous for him. It seems there are tensions between the whites and the coloreds now, especially since so many of them have come into our town. The whites are getting fearful and they're letting their anger control their actions. I think the white folks may be organizing for trouble down there, Micah. There surely is going to be something."

"That's why I have to find Daniel. I don't know what he'll do if he is confronted by coloreds or those other men. Jonathan, I need to get going. If you hear of anything, can you try and get word to me?"

"I will Micah. Just be very careful."

I left Jonathan and headed in the direction of the Baptist Church. It was several blocks away and I was on foot, so I knew it would take me about a half-hour to get there. I wondered what I was would do or say, if I found Daniel. Could I stop him? I didn't know the answer to that but I expected to find out real soon.

Chapter 53

As I approached the colored Baptist Church, I wondered what I would say to Daniel if I found him. Would he be there? Would he listen to me if he was? What would be his state of mind? I didn't have answers to any of those questions.

"Good morning," I said, to a couple of older colored men hanging around at the front of the church as I arrived. "I'm looking for Reverend Thomas. Have you seen him today?"

The two looked at each other and then one replied, "He's inside. I saw him a short while ago."

I pushed open the wooden doors to the church and walked quietly into the sanctuary. I was raised to show respect when in a house of worship.

"Are you here again?" a familiar voice asked. I turned around and immediately saw a friend.

"Millie. It's good to see you again. I'm looking for Reverend Thomas. Is he here?"

"No. He left a little while ago heading toward the river. He said he'd be back later this morning. Do you want to wait for him? I can bring you some coffee and maybe find a biscuit or two."

"No, thank you for offering Millie but I'm really looking for my brother, Daniel. I thought that Reverend Thomas might have seen him. He's tall and slender with light brown hair. Have you seen him?"

"Not around here. I'm sure I would've remembered someone that looked like that, especially here at this church. It's mostly colored folk here as you know. I definitely would've remembered him. Why would he be here?"

"He may be looking for Aliyah. He and Aliyah were close while she was on our farm," I said, but not wanting to get into a discussion about Daniel and Aliyah. "I'll come back in a few hours. Hopefully, the Reverend will be back by then. Have you seen Aliyah?"

"No. I haven't seen her. She may have gone down to the fish market this morning too. She goes there sometimes and helps with cleaning the fish. She may be there now. Women from the church are down there almost every morning doing one thing or another."

"Thanks Millie. I'll be back later." I then left the church and started down toward the river to see what I could find. Maybe I would get lucky and find Daniel and Aliyah together. I didn't have any idea where he could be but I figured I might as well start by looking down there.

It was cool by the river, a damp morning with a light fog hanging in the air. As I got closer to the river, I saw steps that led down to the street below which ran parallel to the river. I stopped for a moment when I reached the cobblestone street and peered in both directions. Two ships were docked nearby to my left, being loaded with cotton. There was activity on other ships to my right with cargo being loaded and unloaded. I saw fishing boats further down to my right so I decided to go that way. One of the larger boats seemed to have quite a bit of activity nearby. I walked closer to get a better look.

"Are you looking to buy fish sir?" a deeply tanned, chiseled faced, elderly man asked me.

"No I'm not. I just wanted to get closer so I could see what was happening. It looks like they had a good morning out on the water. It looks like they caught a lot of fish."

"Yeah, it looks like it. That's my son," he said, proudly pointing to the one directing the activity by the boat. "I used to go out fishing too, until I got too old for it. I miss it though. I loved going out at night, fishing until the early morning hours and coming in and unloading the catch. It was a lot easier before the war though. The boats are getting older now and we can't get the supplies we need to repair them. We have to make do with what we have." He paused, surveyed the scene in front of him and then said again, "Yeah, I miss it a lot."

"I see some colored fellows working over there. Are they here every morning?" I asked.

"Yeah, they help unload the fish and then clean the boats. We usually pay them in fish. Money's in short supply these days as you know. Their women come down here too and help out cleaning fish. I haven't seen them this morning though. I guess they'll be here soon. They use the fish to feed those at their church. They're good workers most of the time but occasionally we'll catch one stealing. Have to be alert for that you know. We have to keep our eyes wide open. Not all of them can be trusted."

"Well, there's good and bad in all people I suppose. I need to be going now. Thanks for talking to me. Good luck today with the catch," I said. I then started walking back in the direction from which I came. After turning away from the street and walking toward the stairs, I heard a barely intelligible voice coming from the shadows of an alley.

"Micah, Micah over here," I heard the voice say. "Come over here."

After a short pause, I recognized that voice. "Daniel, where are you? I can't see you."

"I'm over here behind the barrels."

I walked over toward some used barrels that were standing next to the back of an old red brick building. Even though it was still morning, it was heavily shaded behind the building and not easy to see. "Daniel, why are you hiding?" I asked, as I approached him. "Is someone looking for you?"

"I shot him Micah."

"What? Shot who?" I asked.

"Cartwright. He's dead. I shot him last night."

"You had a duel with Cartwright?"

"No. I waited outside and shot him as he came out of a tavern. I killed him with one shot—right to the heart."

"Daniel, oh my God, why did you do that? The whole town's going to be looking for you. They'll hang you if they find you."

"I know," he said and paused for a moment. "I found Aliyah at the church. I talked with her. She wouldn't come back with me. I was angry and depressed. As I was walking away from the church, I saw Cartwright walking in the distance. I followed him. I saw him go into a tavern and I waited for him to come out. He was no good Micah, you know that. He deserved to die after what he did to me, to us."

I looked at Daniel. I was feeling pity for him. I had never seen him this way before. He looked like he had been up all night. His eyes were red, his clothes were dirty and it appeared that he hadn't shaved in several days. He looked sorrowful.

"You're right, Daniel. He did deserve his due. But now we need to find some place for you to hide. We can't let them find you. Stay here until its gets dark. I'll come back tonight and get you."

"Okay buddy. I'll be right here. Don't forget me."

My mind was spinning. I didn't know where to go or what to do. I had to find a safe place for Daniel to hide but where and for how long? Would anyone help us? I felt my heart pounding as I tried to control my feelings but I knew this wasn't going to be easy. The road ahead had become much more complicated and difficult now. I decided to return to the church.

Chapter 54

As I walked slowly back to the church, I was trying to craft a plan within my spinning mind that would keep Daniel alive. I would seek out Reverend Thomas first. Maybe he would help me. He had to know about Aliyah and Daniel by now, I thought. Surely he would be willing to help.

I reached the church and then walked inside. Millie greeted me. "He's back now Micah. He's in there," she said, pointing to the small room, just past the entrance doors.

"Micah, come in," he said, as I walked into the room. "Millie said you were looking for me. Why are you back so soon? How are you feeling? How's Jesse?"

"I'm okay Reverend. Jesse's getting better. He didn't come with me this time though. I've been looking for my brother Daniel. He came here a few days ago trying to find Aliyah. Do you know about Daniel and Aliyah?"

He looked at me and paused for a moment. "Yes, Aliyah told me. She told me everything. She talked of your farm, her mother, your parents and Daniel."

"Well, I need your help. We need your help."

"I don't understand. How can I help you? Aliyah has asked to stay here Micah. She's not going back with your brother."

"I know. I don't mean that Reverend. Daniel's in trouble. He killed a man. His name was Cartwright. Did you know of him?"

"Yes I did. We've had some issues with him and the Sheriff recently. They seemed to always be hanging around looking for something--looking to stir up trouble. You say Daniel killed him?"

"Yes. He shot him last night. It's a long story that started when we were coming back from the war but he saw Cartwright leaving a tavern and followed him. He's hiding down by the river. If they find him, they'll surely hang him. They probably won't even give him a fair trial. I'm sure they're out looking for him right now. The Sheriff knows they've had run-in's before. I need someplace to hide Daniel until he can get away--where he can lay low for a while. I came here to ask for your help. Will you help me?"

"Micah, it's hard enough just trying to take care of my people and keep up with the daily arrivals. I can't cross the law. I can't risk being shut down. I just can't do it. Can you understand that Micah?" he asked, staring directly at me.

"I don't know what else to do. If they find him they'll kill him. There'll be no justice. When they find him, they'll hang him and the Sheriff will look the other way. I have to do something. Daniel's a good person. He didn't deserve this. I have to try and help him."

"Micah, I'm sorry. I can't help you. It's just too much of a risk for my people and the work I'm doing here."

I got up slowly and walked out of the room. I was sorry and somewhat surprised that Reverend Thomas wouldn't help but I did understand his situation. I didn't know where to turn now. I felt hopeless and without any options.

As I exited a back door of the church, another familiar voice called to me. It was Aliyah. "Micah, what are you doing here? Is something wrong?"

"Daniel's in trouble. I came to see if the Reverend would help. But he won't. He says he can't. I don't know what else to do now."

"What kind of trouble? What are you talking about? I just saw him yesterday. He was upset with me because I wouldn't return to the farm with him but otherwise he was fine."

"Daniel killed that man Cartwright. He followed and then shot him last night as Cartwright was leaving a tavern. Daniel's hiding now. I need to find a place for him to hide for a while or I'm afraid he'll get caught and be hung."

"Micah, I'll talk with Reverend Thomas. Go back to Daniel and bring him back here tonight after it gets dark. I'll help you."

I looked at Aliyah for a moment. I wondered how she could possibly help me if the Reverend said he wouldn't. "But how?" I asked.

Aliyah put a finger to my lips, "Ask no more questions."

"Okay, I'll bring him back later tonight. Thank you Aliyah."

As I headed back toward the river, I knew that Aliyah was my only option now. I had to rely on her to save Daniel. Could we save him? I wondered if Daniel would still be there. Had he already been found? There must be patrols out looking for him, I thought. Can he stay hidden until tonight? I had a lot of questions and few answers but I knew I had to be very cautious returning down to the river.

Chapter 55

I returned to the river just after darkness. I had to find Daniel before Sheriff Billy or any of his buddies did and get him to a safe place.

About three blocks from where I expected to find Daniel, I heard a wagon approaching from behind. I turned back slowly, looking to see who it was.

"Where're you going Micah?" I heard a nauseating voice ask. "Looking for Daniel? You're out after dark. Don't you know it's not safe down here at night?"

"Hello Billy. No, I'm not looking for Daniel. I'm heading down to the river."

"Why are you going there? You know we're looking for your brother. He's a suspect in the murder of Cartwright."

"That's too bad about Cartwright. I just heard about the killing a little while ago. I know they've had some bad blood between them but Daniel wouldn't kill him," I said. "Daniel wouldn't kill anybody."

"I don't know about that. He was a very efficient killer in the war as I remember. He and Cartwright didn't like each other. It makes sense that Daniel might try to kill him after the incident they had in town. Cartwright was shot in the chest. Someone confronted him, then shot him. I need to talk with your brother. Do you know where he is?"

"He's probably back at the farm. I haven't seen him in a few days. I came into town for supplies."

"It seems like you've been coming to town a lot recently. So what are you doing down here anyway? There's not much open at this hour. You're not looking for your brother are you?" he asked again looking at me suspiciously.

"No Billy. I told you that I didn't know where he was. I dropped my pocket watch while I was down here this morning and I was retracing my steps to see if I can find it. It belonged to my father and it means a lot to me."

"Well, I'm looking for Daniel and he may be looking for that slave girl of his. If you see him, tell him I want to talk to him. Oh, if I find your watch Micah, I'll let you know."

"Thanks Billy. I'll be on my way now."

I continued down toward the river but I altered my planned route. I was not going to lead the Sheriff to Daniel. I turned to the right, off the street I was traveling and continued to walk a few more blocks before heading back toward the river. I was being careful in case Billy was trying to follow me. I wondered if he had someone else following me also. I decided to delay a bit, to let it get darker before looking for Daniel.

When it was close to total darkness, other than the few flickering oil lamps along the streets, I headed back to where I thought Daniel should be. I knew it would be dark for a few more hours at least until the moon came up. I approached the back of the building near the barrels where I had last seen him.

"Daniel, Daniel where are you?" There was no answer. "Daniel, are you here?" I waited a few more moments then I started to walk away.

"Micah, I'm over here," I heard him say.

I turned toward his voice. "Where are you?"

"I had to wait and be sure you were alone and not being followed."

"Are you okay?" I asked.

"I'm fine but hungry. I haven't had a bite to eat all day. I had to hide from the searchers who were looking for me. My heart was beating so hard at times that I thought they would find me just by sound of the loud thumping. But I'm okay now. Where are we going Micah?"

"We're going back to the Church. Aliyah said she can help us. There's a place there where you can hide."

"Are you sure it's safe there? I don't think that the Reverend cares too much for me. He looks at me with disgust. I'm not sure he wouldn't turn me in."

"No Daniel, he won't and Aliyah's going to help us. You'll be okay. I trust Aliyah."

"Okay, but I don't trust that Reverend. He might turn me in just to get rid of me."

We headed back to the Church wanting to find Aliyah. She said she would help. I was hoping that she had talked with the Reverend and that he would agree to help us, but I had my doubts. It seemed ironical to me, that Daniel's survival now might depend on the compassion of our former slave girl.

Chapter 56

As we neared the church, I was listening for anything that sounded unusual. I was quite jumpy. It was still very dark, the moon was not up yet and the hazy façade of the church came into view.

"Daniel, I'm going to leave you near the back and go look for Aliyah. Stay here and don't make any noise."

"You don't have to tell me that. I'm the one their looking to find and hang, remember?"

"Okay. Just be still until I return." I turned away from Daniel and started for the door at the rear of the church. The door was closed so I knocked gently.

After a moment or two, the door opened and then I saw Millie. "Is Aliyah here?" I asked in a low tone.

"She's inside. Let me get her."

A few moments later, Aliyah came to the door. "Where is he?" she asked.

"He's over there," I said, pointing to where I had left him a few moments earlier. "We need to hide him. He needs to eat too."

"Bring him in here quickly."

"What about Reverend Thomas?"

She looked at me, paused for a moment then repeated, "Bring him in here quickly. We'll hide him inside."

Within this lovely house of worship, there was also lurking beneath its floors a hidden level. As I looked at the floor, I saw a strange symbol of some kind. I didn't recognize it. I assumed it must be African. I could see small holes in the floor but what I didn't know was that underneath was a hiding area where runaway slaves were kept before making their long journey north on the "Underground Railroad." It was where they could stay out of view and safely hidden until it was time to start their journey to freedom.

Aliyah lifted several planks from the floor and beneath it I could see an area where someone could be hidden. "Daniel, get in there. I'll bring you something to eat in a bit," she said.

Daniel slid awkwardly down through the narrow opening and Aliyah quickly put back the planks she had just removed. She pressed them back into place with her foot until there was no longer any sign of Daniel or his hiding place.

"Are you okay?" I whispered as I kneeled down over the spot where Daniel was now hidden.

"I'm okay but I'm starving. Can someone please bring me something to eat?"

"We'll get something for you but please remain very quiet. Can you do that?"

"Yes, but don't be too long or I may have to start hunting rats."

"Go now," Aliyah said. "We'll take care of Daniel, but be very careful. It's dangerous around here at night."

"I'm going back to the Wright House. I'm sure Jonathan will put me up for the night. Please take care of Daniel. I know they're probably looking for him right now and if they find him they'll kill him without asking any questions."

"We will Daniel. I'll let you know if we need you," Aliyah said.

I looked at Aliyah and nodded my head in approval. I then turned and walked out of the door at the back of the church.

It seemed that Daniel would be safe for now but I needed to find a way to get him out of town and probably out of the state. I felt like I now had a few days to develop a plan but I needed to begin work on it immediately.

Chapter 57

When I reached the Wright House, it was pitch black outside except for a dim-burning lantern sitting on the steps at the entrance. I walked up and knocked on the door. It was not that late, about ten o'clock, so I was hoping that Jonathan would still be up.

"Who is it?" I heard Jonathan ask.

"It's me, Micah. Can you put me up for the night?"

"Micah, okay, give me a moment." He then opened the door. "Sure, I can probably find some space for you. Come on in."

I walked inside and sat down on a chair that was sitting next to the door. "It's been a long day," I said, with a tired voice, wiping the sweat off my forehead with my arm.

Jonathan looked at me then moved a book from the chair where he normally read in the evenings, sitting down next to me by a burning candle on a small table. "I've been reading. Didn't expect any visitors tonight. I always like to read before turning in for the evening. It helps me relax before going to bed. Did you find Daniel? What's going on now? Do you even want to talk about it?

"No, I don't think so Jonathan. I've looked about today but I haven't located him. Maybe he's not here." I hated lying to Jonathan but I didn't want him any more involved than he needed to be. As it stood now, I was protecting a criminal.

"You've been coming here often Micah, although I know you probably didn't expect to have to come here this much. Cassie and Ella must really miss you when you're away?"

"Well, I have a farm and it requires all of my attention to run it. I don't have a lot of money but I can find the things I need here and the people have been helpful to me. They work with me. Cassie and Ella miss me when I'm away but they understand." I paused for a moment and then changed the subject. "Jonathan, I've heard that a man named Cartwright was killed a few nights ago and they're looking for my brother, he's the prime suspect. I overheard Sheriff Billy discussing it today with some townspeople. I stayed out of view but wanted to hear what he was saying."

"I remember that you said they had issues but I never figured Daniel for a killer," Jonathan said, looking at me carefully to see how I would respond.

"Definitely not. They didn't care for each other but Daniel would never try to kill him. Daniel hated the war and he hated the killing that went along with it. I know that Daniel would never do such a thing." I continued to lie to Jonathan but I didn't feel that I could confide in him now. He would be better off not knowing the truth, at least for now, I reasoned.

"Well, they are looking for him Micah, so if you find him you'd better let him know."

"I don't know where he is. He may even be back at the farm right now. That's where I last saw him, a few days ago. He's probably out working in the fields today." I was looking away from Jonathan as I talked with him. I wondered if he was reading my thoughts.

"Sheriff Billy's looking for him and that's for sure. When they get riled up about things around here there's no telling what they'll do. So you'd better let Daniel know if you see him," Jonathan repeated.

"I will. I just hope I find him before Billy does," I said with my voice trailing off. "Jonathan, I may need to stay in town for one more day. I want to be sure that he's not here before I head home. Do you have room for me if I need it?"

"You're always welcome here Micah. As I have said before, I will always find a place for you even if it's in my stable. You'd better get some rest tonight. Go turn in now. I'll see you in the morning for breakfast," Jonathan said.

"Okay. Thanks. You've always been there for me."

"See you tomorrow," he said, walking away and pointing down the hall. "Take number two."

That night I lay awake in bed for several hours. I couldn't sleep. I was turning ideas over and over in my head. Should I try to get Daniel out of town as soon as possible or should he stay hidden for a few more days or even weeks? I wondered if Daniel would be able to hide out on his farm or would he be better off heading west toward Texas? Surely they would find him if he tried to hide at the farm. I knew Billy would continue to hunt him over the next few days and weeks. It would probably be good for me to lay low for a while also. Maybe it was even time for me to leave Savannah and go home.

Chapter 58

I woke up the next morning to the smell of warm biscuits, bacon and brewing coffee. I quickly got dressed and headed to the kitchen. "It smells good in here Jonathan. This is one of the things I miss the most about the war--waking up to a warm tasty breakfast, although truthfully, it didn't happen very often."

"Well, go inside and sit down at the table and I'll have breakfast ready shortly," Jonathan said.

I was the first down this morning so it was quiet sitting at the dining table alone. "You know, Jonathan, the last time I had breakfast here you had that nice couple from Boston sitting at this table. Unfortunately, I don't remember their names."

"Oh, you mean Sally and John Wells. I saw John last week when I was heading down toward the river. He said they've been teaching coloreds near the Negro Baptist Church. John said things were going well but they were short on teaching materials. He said they needed more books, paper, pencils and chalk. I told him I would see what I could do.

"You know, I would like to see them again. Maybe I'll stop by there today if I have time. I'm going to be down that way."

"They're only a few blocks west of the church," Jonathan said.

I finished breakfast, thanked Jonathan and headed out toward the church. I wanted to see how Daniel was doing but I needed to be careful of what I said and where I might be seen. As I neared the church, I decided to go a few blocks to the west. I would look for Sally and John first.

I approached a building that looked like an old grain store. I saw some colored teenage boys hanging around outside so I walked toward them.

"I'm looking for Mister John Wells. Have you seen him?"   "Yeah, he's inside. We're taking a break right now," one of the boys replied.

I walked up the wooden steps. The door was open so I took a look inside. Working at the front of the makeshift classroom was John writing on an old chalkboard. "Hello there, John. Do you remember me?"

He turned around and looked at me. "Sure I do. Micah, isn't it?"

"Yes it is. I stayed with Jonathan last night, had breakfast there this morning and mentioned that I hadn't seen you or Sally in a while and that I wanted to stop by and see you today. He mentioned that you had met last week and he was going to look for some supplies for you. How's it been going?"

"It's been going well. We have about eighteen students now. They range in age from six to about seventeen. You probably saw a few of them, standing around out front. They all have an eagerness to learn so that's been good. We've been spending most of our time teaching them to read and write. Just can't get enough books for all of them. We have to share around here. We need more books and paper to really do it right. How've you been? Did you find that girl you were looking for?"

"Yes I did. She's good. Aliyah is helping out over at the Baptist Church. They've had so many new arrivals to the area that it has been tough for them to stay caught up. Most had been slaves on plantations so being on their own is new to them. It's tough just providing the minimum food and shelter. Aliyah is well though. She seems contented here. I'm happy for her. I think she's found a home."

"I hope they're not having any of the problems we're having here. It seems that some of the white folk in the area don't care much for our teaching the Negro children. We've even had threats that they'd burn down our schoolhouse. I don't know if they would or not but they haven't made it easy for us. We're trying to get the schoolroom established, find supplies and children interested in learning and they want to shut us down. It makes it very hard--darn near impossible. We only want to do some good around here and help out."

"I'm sorry to hear about that. If there is anything I can do to help with your program, please let me know."

"Hi Micah, are you here to learn to read and write?" asked Sally, John's wife, jokingly.

"No, just visiting today although my reading and writing could be improved. It did serve me well though while I was in the army. It helped me to keep up with local newspapers and army regulations."

"If you want to help out, you're welcome anytime," Sally said. "We're teaching reading and writing now but we want to teach arithmetic and geography also. The students who're here are very eager to learn. It's motivating to teach them. I think we're doing important work here, Micah."

"I can see that. Thanks for the offer to help. I may take you up on that. Well, I've got to head over to the Baptist Church now. I want to see Aliyah and say goodbye to her before I head back to the farm. It was really nice seeing both of you again. Good luck with your school."

As I headed toward the church, my memory was quickly jolted back to the reason I was going there. The short visit with John and Sally had, at least for a few minutes, taken my mind off my immediate problems. I wondered, if Daniel was okay. Did the Reverend allow him to stay there? Did he even know? Also, I realized that I needed to be inconspicuous, at least as much as possible, being near a colored Baptist Church. I hoped that I would find Aliyah quickly. Otherwise, I might feel the need to start for home without seeing either of them.

Chapter 59

As I approached the church, I noticed a group of Negroes standing around at the front. I looked for Aliyah but I didn't see her. I did see Reverend Thomas though. He was talking to a group of men and women. At his size, he was hard not to see. I quickly considered that this was probably not a good time for me to be going there. Trying to avoid being seen, I moved behind a tree and made my decision. I would head home instead.

I turned and began to walk away from the church. I hated that I wasn't going to see Aliyah or Daniel before leaving but I was going to trust that Aliyah would take care of him. It was probably good that I not be seen now or draw attention there that could be dangerous for Daniel. I would come back in a few weeks and check on him. For now, I was going home.

About four blocks from the church I heard a familiar voice and one that seemed to be around whenever I was. "Micah, slow down, I want to talk with you."

"Billy Dale. I haven't seen you in a while. I guess I've been lucky," I said, something out of character for me to be saying.

"Screw you, Micah. Where's Daniel? He killed Cartwright you know. Shot him dead. A cowardly act, I would say."

"A lot of people had a reason to kill Cartwright. He was an evil person. But Daniel didn't do it."

"How do you know that? Where is he anyway?"

"He's probably home on the farm where he's been for the last few weeks. Just recently, he's been out and about and started farming again since his injuries. I'm sure he's home working the fields."

"Well, I'm not so sure. Maybe it was you, Micah. You didn't care for Cartwright either."

"That's right. Ever since he robbed us at gunpoint as we were returning from the war, I have had a grudge. Anyone would. But I didn't kill him and Daniel didn't either so you need to start looking elsewhere."

"Well, don't go too far. I may need to see you again."

"I'm going home to my farm. My business is done here. If you need me you can find me there." With that I turned and began to walk away.

"I'm going to find him Micah," I heard Billy say. "I am going to find him."

It was a little while later as I was walking away from town, just starting on the road home, when I heard another familiar voice yelling in the distance. "Micah, Micah wait for me."

I turned back and there she was. "Aliyah," I responded. As she neared, I saw fear on her face. I knew that something bad had happened. "What is it? What's happened?"

"Daniel's gone. He left during the night. He wasn't there this morning. I don't know where he's gone. Nobody saw him leave. He's gone Micah."

"Did he say anything to you?" Why would he leave I wondered. "Aliyah, I'm heading home. Maybe he's there. I'll look for him when I get there."

"They'll kill him if they find him. Please Micah, you have to find him."

"I will. I'll find him Aliyah." I gave her a hug and a kiss on the cheek then turned and started home.

I knew I was running out of time. Why did he leave? Had he gone home? I was hopeful but not very confident that I would find him there.

Chapter 60

I hadn't seen Cassie and Ella for about a week, so I knew they would be excited to see me. "I'm home," I hollered, as I entered the house. But I didn't hear anything. "I'm home," I said again but still no response. I then turned and walked back toward the barn behind our house. I heard Ella laughing so I decided to sneak up on them. "What's so funny?" I asked, as I jumped from behind the side of the barn.

"Father, Father we missed you," Ella said, rushing up to me and giving me a big hug.

"I know my little darling, I missed you too," I said, returning her hug. Then I looked toward her mother who still had dirt on her hands from planting flower seeds behind the house.

"It's about time you came home," Cassie said. "It's tough having to do everything on this farm by myself. I hope you're home for a while this time."

"I am," I replied. "I know I'm behind and there's a lot of work to be done." I gave Cassie a kiss and a big hug and then quietly asked her, "Have you seen Daniel?"

"No. I thought he was in Savannah. I haven't seen him since before you left. You didn't find him there?"

"Yes, I did but I can't talk about it now. We can talk about it after Ella goes to bed."

Cassie gave me a puzzled look. "Okay, we'll discuss it later."

I was glad to be home but I remembered what I had promised Aliyah. My search for Daniel needed to begin but I would wait until tomorrow to start.

After dinner and after putting Ella to bed, I sat down with Cassie. "Daniel killed a man in Savannah."

"What? Why?" Cassie murmured in disbelief.

"Do you remember me talking to you about that fellow Cartwright?"

"You mean the one who robbed you when you were returning from the war?"

"Yes. You also remember the time in Savannah when Daniel jumped from the wagon and began beating up on him. Well, Daniel saw him one evening and followed him to a tavern. When Cartwright came out, Daniel shot him. I found Daniel hiding down by the river and took him to the Negro Baptist Church for hiding. He was there and I thought safe until Aliyah caught up to me as I was leaving town and said he was gone. He didn't give a reason for leaving. He left and no one knows where he is or where he has gone. I know the Sheriff is looking for him but nobody has found him yet. He may have come back here to his farm. I need to try and locate him before the sheriff does. I'll go over to Daniel's place tomorrow morning. I sure hope I find him there."

Cassie was shocked. I could see it on her face. She was aware of his temper but didn't expect anything like this. "He didn't come here. I haven't seen him. Do you think he would've come back, especially knowing that they're trying to find him?"

"I don't know. He may have headed out west. Maybe he's gone to Texas. But I need to look for him," I said.

We stayed awake talking a little longer but it was getting late and I was tired. "Cassie, I'm looking forward to waking up tomorrow and having breakfast with you and Ella. I'm tired now. I need to go to bed. I'm hoping tomorrow is a better day. Good night honey." With that, I turned over and in a short time was in a deep sleep.

Chapter 61

The next morning I got up, had breakfast and headed over to Daniel's place. I didn't know if I would find him but I was hopeful. When I arrived, it looked like he hadn't been there for several weeks. The weeds were tall, overgrowing the front entrance which Daniel normally kept cut and I noticed cobwebs forming inside the window openings. I knew Daniel wouldn't have allowed that because he had a fear of spiders.

I opened the door and slowly entered the house. "Daniel, are you here?" I asked gently. There was no reply. It was a one room living area and I could see quickly that he wasn't there. I walked out and around to the back and headed down to the pond. I thought there might be a chance that he was there though I had little reason now to expect it. As I approached the pond, it was still and quiet. If Daniel wasn't here and it didn't look like he had been, then where was he?

Not seeing him, I decided to head back home. As I was walking back, I saw a familiar face coming my way. It was Jesse. As he got closer, he began running toward me. The expression on his face told me he was about to deliver news that I wouldn't want to hear. I quickly worried that something might have happened to Ella or Cassie.

"They found him," Jesse said. "They found Daniel. He's been shot. He's dead Micah," he said with tears in his eyes. "I'm so sorry."

I felt my heart stop. My immediate thoughts went blank. I couldn't say a word. I was in shock.

"Father's bringing him home now. They found him by the side of the road outside Savannah. He'd been shot several times. They should be home soon," Jesse said.

My thoughts were racing now. I need to get home and tell Cassie. I need to tell her. She needs to know. She'll want to know. I need to get home and tell her right away, I thought.

It's hard for me now to remember the days that followed. We had a small respectful service and buried Daniel in the little cemetery by the church. He would remain for eternity near my father, younger brother, aunts, uncles and cousins who had passed before us. Daniel would've liked it that way and I believed the others would have too. The ordeal was very tough on my mother and I was so grateful that she had Aaron to comfort her.

On day of the service it was dreary out--very hot, humid and overcast. Many of our neighbors came to pay their respects. I spoke briefly at the service by his grave. I talked of Daniel and me growing up on the farm, our time in the war and how lucky we were to have survived when so many others had not. I talked about the difficult conditions we had found when we returned from the war but in spite of that, were truly grateful for the things we still had. I then returned once more to what seemed to me to be the irony of this sorrowful occasion--the war's horrible violence we'd seen and survived and how that incident by the stream that day, as we were returning home from the war had put us on this terrible path. That unexpected act of evil had now resulted in Daniel's death.

"He didn't deserve this," I said, "especially after what he'd been through, fellow soldiers he'd saved and the good life he had always led. But life must go on. Those who remain must help each other through these very difficult times. Things will eventually get better," but I wondered. Would things really get better and when?

The period following Daniel's death was tough for me. I never expected to feel so alone like I did. My father, younger brother and now my older brother were gone. I always thought my big brother would be there for me, always. New thoughts were starting to creep in now. Who did this to him? Was it Billy and his friends? It must have been, I thought. I decided to let that rest and get back to farming for a while. I figured that spending time with the family and doing my daily chores would help things get back to normal. Unfortunately, normalcy didn't last but just a few short weeks.

Chapter 62

It was just after midnight when we heard a soft knock on the door. "Did you hear that Micah?" Cassie asked.

"Yes, I did." I got out of bed slowly and walked toward the front door. I heard the knock again. It was a gentle knock but unmistakable. I opened the door slowly. I saw a familiar face in the darkness.

"Aliyah. What are you doing here?" I asked.

"Micah, there's been trouble. We need your help."

"Micah, who is it?" Cassie asked.

"It's Aliyah," I responded. "Aliyah, what kind of trouble? What do you mean?"

"They burned our school. Everyone is scared. We don't know what to do. Reverend Thomas asked me to come see you. We believe there's more trouble coming. We need you to help us. Will you come back with me?"

"Aliyah, I can't. I'm needed here. Besides, what could I do? I'm just one person. How could I help?"

"You can help us. You were in the army. You know how to handle these things. Will you come back with me?" Aliyah asked again.

"Aliyah, stay here tonight. We can talk about this in the morning. It'll be better to discuss it then."

"I can't, Micah. I have to get back. I have to return tonight while it's still dark. Please come, Micah. We need you." Aliyah then turned and retreated into the darkness.

"Aliyah, wait. Stay here," I called out but she was gone. I felt an ache deep in my stomach. I knew there was no relief for me tonight. I had this feeling that I had to help but I knew Cassie would object. There was no way that she would let me return to Savannah now. Not when she knew there would be real danger. I knew she would be against it. What would I say to her? Could I not go now? Those answers were not going to come easily. I would think on it tonight, I thought. I can decide tomorrow. But I knew I was just kidding myself. I would be up most of the night and I knew the answers would be difficult.

"Micah, what did Aliyah want? Is she still here?"

"Aliyah left. There's been trouble back in Savannah. They need my help."

"You can't go, Micah. I won't let you go."

"We can talk about it in the morning, okay? I'm very tired. I need to rest now."

"You can't go, Micah. That is not your fight. Ella and I need you here. You can't go back. I won't allow it."

"Let's talk about it tomorrow, Cassie. It's late." I got into bed, kissed Cassie on the cheek and rolled over on my side away from her. I was silent but my eyes were wide open, peering into the darkness. What would I say to Cassie tomorrow I wondered? What could I possibly say that would change her mind? I didn't know but I did know that I had to go back to Savannah.

Chapter 63

I got up early the next morning and after a difficult and emotional conversation with Cassie, I was out of the house and on my way. It was troubling leaving my family again. How much longer could I keep doing this? Maybe Cassie was right. Was this really my fight? I was needed on the farm. Not only was I a farmer but also a father and a husband. What if something happened to me in Savannah? How would they survive without me? Who would take care of them? Unfortunately, I didn't have any good answers for those questions. But, I knew I was being pulled back to Savannah by something stronger than myself. I was needed there. I didn't know what I would do when I got there but I knew I had to try to help them.

I traveled all day and made it to Savannah in the early evening. It was just starting to get dark out. I thought about going straight to the church but it might be better to visit Jonathan first and try to get some rest. I would think about my next move over night and start out fresh the next morning.

As I approached the Wright House, I was thinking that it would be good to see Jonathan again. Even though I had seen him a few days earlier, it was always refreshing to see and talk with him. I thought about how things had changed since our last talk. I hadn't been honest with him before about Daniel and now, Daniel was gone and there were unanswered questions about his death. But things were different now, more urgent and tomorrow I would go to the Baptist Church.

I entered the Wright House and knocked on the doorway entrance. "Jonathan, it's me. I'm back again."

"What are you doing back so soon? You must be tired of farming? It must have been all those years of soldiering," he joked. "You're tired of all the dirt, the sweat and the plow."

"No. I still want to be a farmer, Jonathan. I'm still a country boy but, I do like coming here and seeing you. I enjoy our talks together. I've come back this time to assist some friends."

"Who are you talking about, friends?"

I looked up, briefly changing the subject. "What happened to those sky blue curtains you had hanging in the dining area? I don't see them anywhere. They reminded me of the tapestry that you see in books--in the castles of Europe. I liked them Jonathan."

"Oh, they were getting old. I needed to replace them."

"But back to your question, Jonathan. Do you remember that I was looking for Aliyah, the slave girl who lived on our farm?

"Yes, I remember."

"I found her Jonathan. She's working down at the Negro Baptist church. They've been helping the former slaves and others who've come into town to find food and shelter. They also need to help them find work. Some need medical care too. The church does good work down there Jonathan. You should go see for yourself."

He looked at me and nodded. "You said you needed to assist some friends."

"You remember John and Sally Wells don't you? They were the ones who stayed here and I met them at breakfast on an earlier visit."

"Sure, I remember them."

"Well, they opened a small school for Negroes not far from the church and they've been teaching there for several months. Mostly, they've been teaching them to read. The other night, Aliyah came to see me at the farm. She said their building was badly damaged by fire by a group of marauders on horseback. She said she couldn't tell who they were because their faces were covered with hoods. She asked me to help them. I'll tell you Jonathan, I don't know what I can do but I feel that I must try to do something."

"Isn't that dangerous Micah? Working with the Negroes could put you in harm's way. I hear rumors of more violence coming. The people, I mean the white people, don't want them here. I think that's a very serious situation you're getting involved in. You might get hurt, even killed. I hope you'll reconsider this before you act."

"I know you're concerned about me Jonathan but it's something I have to do. It wouldn't be right not to try."

"Micah if you have to do it, then at least try to be safe about it. For God's sake man, you have a wife and child. It would be a tragedy if something were to happen to you. Please try to be careful."

"I will Jonathan. I plan to rest here tonight, if you'll have me and then go down to the church tomorrow. I also want to find Sally and John and see if I can help them repair their school."

"These are very dangerous times Micah. Be careful where you go and who you're seen with down there. A lot of people are watching. You can't trust anyone." He paused, "Micah, I meant to tell you earlier how sorry I was to hear about your brother. I liked him a lot. You both helped me in my time of need. I was sorry to hear about him."

"Thank you Jonathan. I appreciate your thoughts. How did you hear?"

"They said his body was found beside the road outside of town. Sheriff Billy told me."

"I'll tell you Jonathan, after what we'd been through in the war, I never expected anything like this to happen. I expected to return to a quiet life of farming. While I'm in town, I want to see Sheriff Billy and see what more he can tell me. I want to get to the truth about Daniel's death. There's got to be more to it than what they're saying."

"Billy mentioned it to me a day after it happened. He said a farmer coming in to town found his body. He brought Daniel here. Billy said he thought it might be related to the murder of that guy, Cartwright. I don't know any more about it than that Micah. It's a damn shame though. I know Daniel was a good man. He'll be missed. Why don't you go get a bath and then come back down to the kitchen? I'm sure I can find something for you to eat. We had ham and potatoes earlier this evening. I'll warm you up some leftovers."

I looked at Jonathan and nodded in agreement. I had talked with him about my business more than I had intended to but I felt he deserved to know the truth. It seemed like the right thing to do. I couldn't continue lying to him. I decided it was now time to look ahead to tomorrow and do what I could to get some rest.

Chapter 64

I was up early the next morning, had a bite to eat and started walking toward the church. I wanted to find Aliyah first and let her know that I had come to help. She seemed so stressed when she came to the farm asking for my help.

On my arrival at the church, I went directly inside. At first I didn't see anyone and then I saw what appeared to be smoke and fire damage on one of the walls. I slowly walked over to it.

"Do you see what they did last night? We got lucky," Aliyah said. They tried to burn down the church and they would have if we hadn't put out the fire so quickly. Hooded riders threw torches through the windows. We don't know who they were but they meant to do us harm."

"Are you okay?" I could see a large bruise on Aliyah's right arm and signs of bleeding on her clothes.

"I was outside when they rode up. One of them hit me with his gun. He tried to hit me in the face but I moved my arm in front to block him just before he swung at me. There were others with him."

"How many were there?"

"About eight or ten, I think. They said they would come back. They said they didn't want us in their town and they were going to take it back. They were hateful men, Micah."

"Where is Reverend Thomas?" I asked.

"He's out back. They're cleaning up from last night. The Reverend is getting some folks together today to talk about what happened last night and what we need to do."

"What does he mean to do?"

"They want to be ready next time. They want to fight back if attacked again."

"Do you know if you have any weapons?"

"No, I don't know. But we need to do something."

I decided to walk outside and find the Reverend. He was working on a table that looked like it had been broken in the attack.

"What do you want white man?" an unknown voice asked, as I walked toward the Reverend.

"I'm looking to talk with Reverend Thomas," I replied, to an angry-looking man holding a hammer.

"It's okay," Reverend Thomas said. "I know this man. Micah, I see you're back. What do you want?" he asked in a kindly manner.

"I've come to see if I can help. Aliyah asked me to come back. She thought maybe I could be of help."

"We don't need your help Micah. We can take care of this ourselves," he said in a defiant voice.

"I've made some contacts around town. I think I can help if you'll let me. I was in the army during the war. Please let me try."

"You can help by staying away Micah. We don't need you."

"It's dangerous now. They won't stop at just last night's attack," I said. "They'll be back. I can help. I'll leave for now but I'm coming back. I can't leave Aliyah here while there's danger."

"We'll take care of Aliyah. Now go," he said.

I looked at him for a moment then turned and walked away. At the front of the building I saw Aliyah.

"What did he say," she asked.

"He told me to leave. He said they didn't need me. I'm leaving now but I'm coming back. Tell the Reverend that I mean to help and I will be back. I'm going now to find someone who can help us."

I looked at Aliyah then walked away. The day was still early and I had work to do. My first stop would be at the Freedman's Bureau.

Chapter 65

My first task was to find out what help was available for the colored community. Were all available resources being utilized? Did anyone on the outside really care? It didn't seem so to me. At the Freedman's Bureau, I hoped to find out what they were doing and if they could help prevent the violence that was occurring.

Within the colored community, life was very tough anyway. Jobs, food and housing were difficult to acquire if not, non-existent for new arrivals. Medicine was lacking and treatment was not readily available for diseases and sickness as the need might suggest. The church was doing what it could with temporary housing and assistance but the numbers were growing and the task becoming overwhelming.

I arrived at the Bureau at about ten o'clock in the morning. From the outside, the old wooden building looked like an abandoned hardware or feed store. As I walked inside, there was a musty smell that was probably caused by the building being vacant for a while.

"Can I help you sir?" asked a friendly voice from across the room. "I'm Gerald Scott. I run the office here in Savannah. And, with whom do I have the pleasure of speaking?"

"My name is Micah Boden. I have a farm about fifty miles southwest of here. I've been trying to help my friends over at the colored Baptist Church."

"I know Reverend Thomas. We've been providing the church with food for the new arrivals. They're doing a wonderful job down there. But it seems they need more and more as the weeks go by. Did he send you over to request more food and supplies? What does he want?"

"No, he didn't send me. I'm here on my own. They're having more and more violence against their community and I wanted to see if there's anything that can be done about that."

"Why do you want to help? What is your connection to them?"

"We had two female slaves working on our farm and one of them is in town now helping at the church. She came to me the other night to request my help against the violence. It seems that the local whites are causing more and more trouble for them. As you may already know, they badly damaged the school building several nights ago and last night they tried to burn down the church. I had military experience in the war and I wanted to see if I can help them."

"Well, it may not be the locals causing the trouble. It may be outsiders. Have you been over to the Military District? If there's recurring trouble maybe they can help you. I see Colonel Alexander almost every week. My efforts here consist of trying to get the white plantation owners and the colored workers to agree on terms for working together--contracts. The coloreds get paid for their labor now, which is not at all like it used to be. Most plantation owners don't even want us here. They would have the Negroes starve and force them to accept lower wages if they could. I also help provide learning materials for the Negroes. They need and desire education and I try to assist with that. We also provide as much food and supplies as we can. Our normal daily rations include bacon, cornmeal and molasses. I dare say though that our supplies are limited at times."

"Can you provide weapons to them so they can protect themselves?" I asked.

"That's not our mission. The local Sheriff or the military would have to handle that. We've had violence to our schoolhouses recently but we ask the Military for protection when it happens. We're not in the protection business Micah."

"Well, Mr. Scott you've been helpful. Thank you for the information. I think I'll take a walk now and see if I can find Colonel Alexander at the Military District."

"Okay. Good luck with your efforts Micah."

With that I turned and walked out the door. I could tell that Scott was aware of the recent violence and he seemed sensitive to the question of who could provide help. I was hoping that just maybe, Colonel Alexander would be able to provide some answers to my questions and useful assistance.

Chapter 66

I didn't have to walk far to find the military district office. The office was around the corner and about three blocks down the next street. The war was over but the Congress had determined that a military presence was still needed in the Southern states to re-establish local and state governments and provide security for the communities as the freedman and the white citizens were integrated culturally in a vastly different way.

The local office had occupied an abandoned home. It was white with a porch that surrounded the front and one side of the building on the first and second floors of the house. It was a bit rundown with visible cracks in the plaster and paint was peeling on the outside of the house but I could imagine the pride the family who previously occupied it must have felt back in the 1850's.

There were two guards posted outside the door as I approached. "What is your business here sir?" a young private asked.

"I would like to see Colonel Alexander," I stated.

"Is he expecting you?"

"No, but I need to see him. It's very important. Can you see if he will meet with me please?"

"What is your name sir?"

"My name is Micah Boden. Please tell him I have come quite a ways to see him."

The guards looked at each other briefly and then the soldier who had been asking the questions turned and walked inside.

The private soon returned. "Colonel Alexander will see you shortly. Wait here."

"Thank you."

After about five minutes a tall man in a military uniform appeared at the door. "Are you Mr. Boden?"

"Yes sir. I'm Micah Boden."

He looked at me for a moment, briefly surveying me and I assumed, deciding if I looked respectable. "Come with me. It's time for my daily walk. You don't mind doing business as we walk do you?"

"No Colonel, I don't."

"I usually walk down by the river every morning. It helps to clear my head and get my thoughts straight and it has a calming influence on me."

"I'm a farm boy," I said. I have a wife and daughter about fifty miles southwest of here. Since the war ended things have been tough on the farm and the weather hasn't been helpful. At best we're struggling to get by."

"I know it's been rough. I've seen how the war has changed the South. It'll be decades before things are like they were before the war. I'm just trying to keep the peace down here, trying to keep the whites from killing the Negroes. It's been tough. The whites are not cooperating. Violence is a daily occurrence. It doesn't seem like the local Sheriff cares much to prevent it either. He's been very uncooperative. Just between you and me, I may have to remove him soon. I'm getting some bad reports about him."

"You're talking about Billy Dale aren't you Colonel? I know him from the war. We served in the same unit together--the 54th Georgia Infantry."

"I know that unit. I fought against you at Kennesaw Mountain. I commanded an Illinois regiment. We went against Loring's Corps. You were in Hardee's Corp I believe."

"That's correct Colonel. You have a good memory. That was a tough day. I still think about the war every day and probably always will."

"Well, I've been doing most of the talking. How can I be of help to you Micah?"

"I'm trying to help the Negroes at the Baptist Church. They're seeing some vandalism and violence over there and they asked me to help. I wanted to talk with you to find out what can be done."

"That's interesting Micah. How did you get involved? You fought on the side to preserve slavery. Why do you care now? Most whites down here seem to be on the other side of the fence. They don't want the coloreds in their town."

"My family had two slave women working for us on the farm. I grew up with them. My brother, now deceased, had a relationship with the younger one. She's now in Savannah working at the Baptist Church. She came to see me one night and asked for my help. They see the violence growing and they're scared. They don't know what to do about it. Because I care for her, I wanted to try to do something. I visited the Freedman's Bureau before I came here and Mr. Scott suggested that I see you. I want to see what can be done before things get even worse."

"I'm afraid things will get worse Micah. That's one of the reasons I'm here. But it's tough to stop the violence. Most of it occurs at night and it's tough to identify who's doing it. It seems they wear hoods or masks. Some are even wearing sheets. We don't know who they are but we want to stop them. Micah, go back to them and tell them to take precautions. Tell them to stay off the streets at night, especially the women. Tell them to stay indoors if possible. If they can identify anything, that would be helpful. Maybe they've seen a person that they recognize; maybe a horse that they've seen on the streets; maybe the way someone talks or moves, anything that could be helpful to us should be reported."

"Can you give us weapons to defend ourselves Colonel?"

"Micah, that's something I can't do. You must know that. But, if you hear of anything or you can identify anybody involved, come see me right away. You be careful. There are a lot of whites out there who aren't going to be happy with what you're doing."

As we returned back to his headquarters, I told him I appreciated his help and the information he'd provided. He told me to be patient; that we would get the people responsible for the violence.

I thanked the Colonel then walked away. I decided to go back to the church. I didn't feel like I had accomplished much this morning but I did get to meet the people that I needed to know and what they could or couldn't do for us going forward. My challenge now would be to convince the reverend to let me help him and the others. That would be a very big challenge.

Chapter 67

It had been quiet at the Church for several nights and the normal work of helping new arrivals settle in to the community continued. Aliyah had talked with Reverend Thomas while I was away and he agreed to let me stay there a few nights if I did some work around the church. I agreed knowing that I could probably patch holes in the roof or floor and work in the vegetable garden behind the church. These were chores I performed at home so I was at least familiar with them.

One night, I had stayed up a little later than most when I heard horses coming in the direction of the church. I recognized those sounds as being similar to what I had heard during the war, that of approaching cavalry. I was sitting out behind the church so I moved up closer to the street where I could take a look. I saw a group of about ten men on horses riding quickly past the church and down toward the area where new arrivals had been living. I saw torches being thrown and heard the crack of guns being fired. There were screams and panic as the victims reacted to the surprise attack. I rushed down toward the screams. I hid behind a wall and peered out toward the commotion.

The torches had landed, huts were burning and I thought I could make out dark figures lying on the ground. After a few minutes, the firing stopped and I could see the attackers riding away. It was too dark for me to recognize any of them but I could see the carnage and destruction they had left behind.

"Oh my God, what's happened?" I heard a voice say. It was Reverend Thomas and he raced by me not waiting for an answer. I followed him as he rushed toward the burning shacks and the fallen bodies on the ground.

"Who did this? Why would they do this?" he asked in a pained voice.

Others were coming now. Buckets of water were thrown on the burning huts. Aid was being provided to those who had been shot or struck by a weapon. I counted at least six huts burning and five victims lying on the ground.

I saw three of the victims getting up slowly covered with blood on their clothes and bodies. I walked over and examined the two not moving, a man and a woman. I had seen these types of wounds during the war and I knew they probably wouldn't survive the night.

"Micah, they keep coming back. Why are they doing this?" Aliyah asked.

I pulled her close and tried to comfort her. "These are hateful people. They're not capable of compassion. Someone has to stop them or they'll continue this violence. I wish I knew who they were. I saw them from a distance but couldn't recognize them. Some wore masks and others wore hoods. They must be from around here because they knew where they were going and what to target. I have to find out who they are."

The next morning, I again went to see Colonel Alexander at the district office. I wanted to tell him what had happened and what I saw last night hoping he could help us.

"I'm here to see Colonel Alexander," I said as I walked up to the guards in front of the district office. I had a very serious look about my presence and the guard seemed to sense that.

"Wait here, sir, I'll see if he's available."

A few moments later, Colonel Alexander appeared at the door. "Micah, come in. Let's talk. What do you have for me?"

"They've struck again Colonel. I didn't get a close-up look but there appeared to be about ten of them and they wore masks and hoods. I saw some with torches and others with pistols and shotguns. It was dark but I could see by the light from their torches. They raided the huts where the church is providing shelter for newcomers. Several were burnt down. Two individuals living there were killed. More were injured. The people are afraid. They don't know what to do or where to go. A bad situation is getting worse down there. Can you help us Colonel?"

"If I knew who they were, I would. The Sheriff should be doing more but he acts like he doesn't know anything about it or who's involved. This has been going on for several weeks now. I wish I could do more Micah but I need more information before I can act."

"Colonel, we still need weapons. Can you give them to us? I could show them how to use them and at least we could fight back. These attackers are nothing but hooded cowards attacking those who are defenseless. We need to stand up to them."

"No, I can't do that Micah. I can't allow a war within my district. No, I need to find another solution. I'm going to talk with the Sheriff and see if I can get any information from him. I'll tell you honestly, Micah, if he won't talk, I'll relieve him from his duties. I can't allow this violence to continue."

"Thank you Colonel but a few pistols or rifles could surely help us more."

"I know Micah but I can't do that. I'll do what I can, I promise you."

I nodded to the Colonel and then departed. There was more that needed to be done but I wasn't sure what to do next. I decided that it was time for me to visit my friend Jonathan at the Wright house again. Maybe he could shed some light on who's behind the violence.

Chapter 68

I spent the next morning working at the church and then left to go see Jonathan that afternoon. If there was anyone in town who knew what was going on and what the people were thinking it was surely him. I wanted to talk with him and see if I could get any information that would be helpful to our cause.

I was on my way to the Wright House, when I heard a familiar voice call out, "Micah." I looked back and saw that it was Billy Dale.

"Billy, it's been a few days. I was hoping to see you."

"I'm sorry about your brother. I'm sure you miss him. He was a good soldier."

"Yeah, I do. Billy, what do you know about his killing? I'm sure you've investigated. I hear it was clear and simple murder. I'm looking to find out more details. The killer or killers need to be caught."

"They found his body on the road that leads out of town. It must have been drifters. We've had problems here with them since the end of the war. They just don't seem to understand that the war's over. They don't have anywhere to go, anything to do so they just look for trouble. I arrest them all the time around here. They're like roaches. You can't get rid of them."

"Why do you think it was drifters? Couldn't it have been someone locally who just wanted to get even? Maybe it was one of Cartwright's friends. They may have thought Daniel was his killer. I know that Daniel created some enemies in town on more than one occasion. I really think it may have been someone other than drifters Billy. You should check that out."

"Be careful what you say Micah and who you say it to. There are people in town that don't want to be falsely accused. With anger boiling over in town right now, anything could happen. By the way, why are you back in town? I thought you were a farmer. Don't you need to work your fields?"

"I come to town every few weeks for supplies and to see friends."

"I heard you may be in town looking for your former Negro slave. Maybe you're trying to help her. That wouldn't be very smart Micah. Things are happening and you don't want to be caught up in them. You should mind your own business and get out of town. You have a wife and child to care for and you need to get back to them."

"Why are you so interested in what I'm doing Billy? Don't you have other things to worry about?"

"I like you Micah. We served together. We fought side by side during the war. Seeing what we had to go through, I just wouldn't want anything to happen to you now. You don't know this town like I do. It's very dangerous around here. You need to go home Micah."

"Well, thank you Billy. I appreciate your interest but I can take care of myself. I have a little more business here and then I'm heading home. But thank you for your advice."

"No problem, Micah. I care only for your well-being," he said with an awkward smile.

I looked at him and slowly turned and walked away.

The journey to the Wright House took only a few more minutes. I entered the front door and called out for Jonathan.

"He's in the kitchen. I'll get him for you," said Lettie, who was cleaning the room closest to the entrance.

"Micah, welcome. You're becoming one of my regular customers. What brings you to town this time? What can I do for you?"

"I just wanted to talk with you. You seem to know what's going on in town. I need to get some answers."

Jonathan limped over to a chair and sat down. "Oh, that feels good. I needed to sit for a few minutes."

"How's that going?" I said, pointing to his disabled legs.

"I have pain most of the time but I can still get around. It doesn't hurt to have a bottle of whiskey handy just in case. It helps me get through the day if you know what I mean. What else am I going to do?"

"Jonathan, what do you know about the mood of the people in town? There have been raids in the Negro areas by unidentified individuals wearing hoods and masks. Have you heard anything?"

"Why are you asking me that, Micah?"

"I told you earlier that Aliyah is living and working at the church and I'm concerned for her safety. That's it. If I can help her in any way, I want to try."

"The people of this town are good Micah. They wouldn't do anything evil to the Negroes. But they're upset with what's happening here. They feel that their being overrun by the colored outsiders, especially those who left the plantations. They're coming here from all over Georgia and beyond. We can't care for them all Micah, do you understand? It shouldn't be our problem. We don't have the resources."

"But that's no reason for the violence. Who could be causing the trouble? Who are the leaders? Have you heard anything Jonathan?"

"I try not to get involved Micah. I just run my house and go to church on Sundays. I'm a good citizen. That's all I can tell you."

"I saw Sheriff Billy a little while ago. I think he knows more about Daniel's murder than he's saying. I think it was probably Cartwright's friends who killed Daniel. They probably did it to get even. They may have thought Daniel killed him.

"That Sheriff Billy, he's a secretive one. He probably knows more than he's saying but I don't think he was involved with the death of your brother."

"How can you be so sure? I know he was looking for Daniel and he didn't like him either. I still have my doubts about the Sheriff. I'm thinking he might have been involved too."

"Well, be careful Micah. There's more going on in this town than you're aware of and you need to watch out. Do your business and go back to the farm. It'll be safer there."

"Okay. Thanks for the information and your concern for me. I'll finish up my business and then head home." As I left the house, I thought it was interesting that Jonathan had said to me almost the same thing that Billy had.

Heading back to the church, I wasn't sure if I had gained any additional information but I did have a sense that Billy knew more than he had said and that maybe, Jonathan wasn't being totally open with me either.

Chapter 69

It seemed like the raids at night were happening now with more frequency. Attacks would come by a band of about ten to fifteen men at different areas of the Negro community. Huts would be burned or badly damaged and in some cases, Negroes beaten up or worse. Something needed to be done to discourage or stop these attacks. I wasn't sure what would work but I wanted to put together a plan. I had met with both the Military District and the Freedman's Bureau but neither seemed to have been of much help. Both were doing what they could but it wasn't nearly enough.

"Where's Reverend Thomas?" I asked, as I entered the side door of the church.

"He's out back," someone replied. I started out toward the back of the church and saw a group of men standing around with the pastor. I walked up quickly behind them. Reverend Thomas saw me coming.

"Micah, come here. What do you want?"

"I want to help. I've been to see the military and the Bureau and I don't see much help coming from them. We need to do something to protect this community. I think I can help if you'll let me."

As I talked, I noticed several fellows looking at each other with doubt on their faces. "I have military experience. We need to come up with a plan. We need one now. I want to help you. Please let me," I said, looking around slowly at different individuals in the group.

Reverend Thomas stared at me for what seemed like minutes and then said, "Okay, what's your plan?"

We spent several hours together that evening and when we broke up our gathering, I felt we had come up with something that might work. It would take time, some training, a lot of effort and whatever resources we could find. But I felt it would be worth it.

Our plan of action was put together over the next few days and nights. Pickets were located at key points around the Negro community and they were posted every night when the sun went down. For this role, we selected fast runners who would come quickly and alert us when they heard the horses coming.

We set up an internal contact system whereby the communication would branch out like the limbs on a tree. Each person alerted would contact two others and continue until everyone was notified. Our gathering point was located behind the church.

We found men in our group who had carpenter and blacksmith experience and we put them to the task of making throwing weapons such as spears and hammers that could be used against our attackers. Our resources were limited but we used everything we could find in our immediate area. The weapons would be primitive but they could still get the job done.

Our reaction force numbered about thirty men, who would respond quickly to our alert system. I trained them in small unit tactics and maneuver similar to what I practiced with the 54th Georgia. The goal was to cut off and isolate our intruders and then assault them from the sides and rear. I felt we were ready after several rehearsals but we hadn't been tested by an actual assault. Although no one within the group besides myself had prior military experience, the will to at least do something and protect their loved ones was a strong motivating factor for everyone.

It had been several days since the last raid. We were thankful for that because it gave us time to test our alert system and correct problems that needed to be fixed. It also gave us time to manufacture our weapons.

We knew there would be another attack. We just didn't know when. I couldn't be sure if our plan would work but I knew that to do nothing would be even more dangerous and tragic.

Chapter 70

It was a warm, humid night out and there was no moon to be seen. The rain had come down hard, earlier in the evening and it was one of those nights where you probably didn't want to be outside for very long. I was inside the church talking with Reverend Thomas and several others about the older members in the community and what additional assistance we could provide when the door suddenly slammed open. Johnny, a young man who was posted at one of our furthest listening points by the main road, came rushing in breathing and panting very heavily. "Their coming, their coming," he shouted with eyes as large as saucers.

"Quick now, get up and pass the alert," the Reverend shouted at a startled young fellow who had been dozing in the corner of the room. The teen was up like a flash and out the side door of the church racing quickly to his designated contacts.

"Let's go," I said to Reverend Thomas. We had picked a spot earlier in the day, near the front of the church and within some large bushes where we could see down the road and direct our reaction team. We would be in danger however if spotted, so I was determined that we would stay hidden from view.

"They're coming, over there," I said, pointing several hundred yards to our front. We could see torches and hear the pounding of horse hooves in the distance. The sound and the blurry view of riders in the distance was coming closer and becoming clearer. I wondered if the church would be their target. It appeared so as they continued coming in our direction galloping faster as they approached.

"We're here sir," I heard the reaction team leader say.

"Okay, I replied. Move your teams to both flanks of the church as we practiced." We had previously prepared moveable barriers, some were old church benches and placed them on all sides of the church, about fifty yards away so they could be moved quickly to block off portions of the roads leading to or past the church as the action required.

As they came closer, I could see them more clearly. They were wearing white hoods so I couldn't identify them.

"There's the church. Let's burn it to the ground," I heard their leader shout. He was wearing a flowing blue cape and a hood covering his face. I could see all the raiders now, most were clutching weapons and others were carrying torches.

As they moved closer toward the church, the riders stayed bunched together. They assumed they were attacking a sleeping community caught by surprise on a rainy, dreary night. They were wrong and we were ready.

I saw several torches thrown to the top of the church roof and others through the windows on the side of the building. It wouldn't take long before the church would be burning, I thought. Inside the church, Aliyah and the others were hiding. Pots of water had been placed within the church at various locations in case of fire. That now seemed to be a very wise decision. Hopefully, they could react to the torches quickly and contain the fires before they spread.

Bam, bam, bam, I heard as shots were fired. I didn't know if anyone had been hit. The teams began moving the barriers into the street behind the attackers. Our plan was unfolding. The raiders didn't see the barriers slipping in behind them.

It was primitive weapons and tactics versus a civil war type raiding party, I thought. The first wave of our reaction team, about twenty men were at the riders quickly after the first shots were fired. They threw their spears and clubbed their mounted enemy before they could respond. I heard additional firing now and I saw two colored men fall to the ground.

A second, similar sized team charged from the opposite direction hurling their spears and swinging their clubs. I saw two of the raiders' horses fall to the ground and several of the attackers were now on the ground being struck repeatedly with clubs. I heard more shots. I saw more of our guys drop. It reminded me of a hand-to-hand skirmish during the Atlanta campaign. Our plan was unfolding violently.

"Let's get the hell out of here," I heard someone yell. I looked up and it was the attacker in the blue cape making his escape. He seemed to be riding awkwardly on his horse as he made his retreat. As he passed near me, I raced toward him from the side. He fired at me with his pistol and I felt a sharp pain in my shoulder but I kept running toward him. I leaped up, over his horse and knocked him off. Just as I went to grab him, Reverend Thomas hit him two hard blows with his club. The attacker in blue groaned and became silent.

Some of the attackers had escaped but most were still on the ground left behind. We had caught eight of them.

I looked down at the one who had been wearing the blue cape. I grabbed his hood and ripped it off. I was stunned. It was Jonathan.

I lifted him up. Blood was running down the side of his head but he was conscious. "You, why you Jonathan?"

He looked up at me and responded quietly. "This is my home. This is our town. They have no right to be here. We had to stop them."

I looked at him in disbelief then lowered his head back down. I got up and walked away.

Inside the church I could see fire. I saw motion as those inside were hurrying about. Luckily the torches thrown on to the roof had rolled off and didn't catch fire.

"Aliyah, where are you?" I looked around inside. Smoke filled the large room. I covered my mouth as I began to cough. At the front entrance I saw her swatting a small fire with a broom and helping others to extinguish it. I rushed over to help her. After a few minutes, the small fires were out. It appeared that several rows of pews had been burned and there was some fire damage to the side of one wall but that seemed to be the extent of it.

"Thank goodness you're okay Micah. Those men were awful," Aliyah said.

"There are men hurt outside. We need to check on them."

"Let's go," she said, grabbing my arm.

"Micah, it looks like you had quite a fight here tonight," I heard a voice in the dark say, as I walked toward the injured men. I looked to my right. Colonel Alexander and a group of soldiers were standing nearby.

"We were ready for them Colonel. I think we showed them something. They were nothing but cowards striking at those who couldn't defend themselves. I think we got their leader," I said, pointing to Jonathan still lying on the ground.

"We'll take him and the others with us. You did well tonight, Micah. How's your shoulder?" the Colonel asked.

I looked down at my right shoulder and noticed blood seeping from a wound. I had forgotten that I had been shot. "I think I'll be okay. It's just a graze."

We were lucky that evening. No one was killed but about five of our lads were wounded. I felt good that we had defended the church and the community. Who would have expected it? Certainly the raiders didn't. But I had lost a friend, Jonathan. I hadn't expected that. The military took him away that night and I never saw him again.

Chapter 71

I stayed in town a few more days helping to clean up around the church and providing additional information to Colonel Alexander. Jonathan and several others had been arrested the night of the raid. Amongst those were a local lawyer, two store owners and Billy Dale. I wasn't sure what the military would do with them but I felt like the actions we had taken would put them away for a while. Hopefully, it would at least make others think about it a little more before they tried it again. I hoped we had bought some time and respect by our actions.

I enjoyed spending time with Aliyah again. For many years on the farm we had played and worked together and usually side by side, planting and harvesting. As always, she maintained her good humor, easy-going temperament and was a pleasure to be around. I knew I would miss her when I departed.

"How much longer will you be here?" Aliyah asked.

"I'll remain a few more days then I'll need to start home. I've left Cassie and Ella alone for far too long now. There's plenty of work for me to do when I get home."

"We'll miss you. We couldn't have done it without you Micah. I overheard Reverend Thomas saying last night that you must have been sent by God. Several heads nodded in agreement when he said that. But I've known that since we were kids on the farm. I always thought there was something special about you Micah, both you and Daniel. I sure do miss him. It was a shame he was taken from us."

"I know. I miss him too, very much. How could we not?"

A few days later I packed up what little things I had and got ready to leave town. I had arranged to catch a ride home with a neighbor that I'd seen in town.

"You're not going to leave without saying goodbye are you?" I heard a booming voice shout.

I turned around and saw Reverend Thomas. "No, I couldn't do that."

"We're sure going to miss you around here. I think we'll be okay though. You've got us going in the right direction now. I think we can take care of ourselves."

"They may be back. It may be next week or next month or next year but they'll return."

"We'll be ready for them," he said.

"Keep everyone together Reverend. You're doing good work here, God's work and the community needs you to keep it going. There's still challenging times ahead of us, I'm sure of that. Things are tough but I know they'll get better." I paused, "It's time for me to leave now. I have to go home to the farm. I've got a lot of catching up to do."

"We'll miss you Micah and we'll never forget you and what you did. You're always welcome to stop by when you're in town. In fact, I'll be upset if we don't see you from time to time. Goodbye Micah," the Reverend said.

My ride was waiting on me and we had a long day ahead of us. I was eager to get started. I gave Aliyah a hug and told her I would see her again soon. Coming to town to the market or for supplies was necessary so I expected to see everyone again in a few months if not sooner.

As we pulled away from the church I looked back. I waved and thought about what we had accomplished in just a short span of time and of my many new friends. I would miss Aliyah greatly for she was like a sister to me. I also wondered about those who had attacked the church and had gotten away. Would we be seeing them again? But this was not the time for those thoughts. I had my wife and child to look forward to and the rest of our lives together.

Chapter 72

I made it home later that night and I was so excited to see Ella and Cassie again. I had been away much too long and I had a lot of work ahead of me. As I walked in the door, Ella ran up and gave me a long hug. I realized then, that I could never stay away for that long again. It was too painful. I missed them too much. Also, I knew that I was very lucky to have returned home safely from Savannah.

"You've got a lot of work ahead of you mister," Cassie said. "The roof needs patching and I need attention. We haven't seen you in a while you know." She paused, "What happened to your shoulder?"

"It's okay, just a scratch. It will be better in a few days."

"You'd better let me take a look at that and make sure it's healing properly."

"Okay. It's still sore, so please be careful. I'll start on those other things as soon as I can." I cleaned up that evening, had a small bite to eat and then went straight to bed as the long day had worn me out. I could begin work on the projects tomorrow, I thought. But now I needed some rest.

The next few weeks were for catching up. There was work to be done on the roof and the barn and I needed to begin harvesting the maturing cotton. The days were warm and long but there was an occasional hint of autumn coming our way in some of the gentle northern breezes.

One night, as we began our evening meal and had just said grace, a rain shower started and I noticed that rain was coming in from an open window. "I'd better close that," I said, and I quickly got up from the table and went over to the window.

Cassie observed me for a moment and saw that I was having a problem closing it, so she came over to help. "Did you leave your muscles in Savannah?" she asked jokingly. "Here, let me help you with that," and she gently pushed me to the side. "The corner gets stuck sometimes."

At that moment, there was a loud crack and I was showered with blood. Cassie had been shot. She fell to the ground and as I tried to sit her up, I could see that she had been hit by a bullet in her upper arm. I grabbed a rag that was hanging nearby and covered the slowly bleeding wound. Ella was crying and I tried to calm her.

"Mother is okay. She'll be okay Ella. Can you see her? She's looking at you."

Cassie then looked up at me and said, "I love you both Micah, so much," and closed her eyes.

"You'll be okay Cassie. I saw wounds like this during the war and I know you'll be okay. It'll hurt for a while but you'll get better, I promise."

I was reacting to the moment but I was still in shock. I laid her down for a moment and ran over to the door to take a look outside. I could hear a horse riding away but it was too dark to see anything. I closed the door and returned to Cassie's side. She was looking at me with an easy smile.

"I guess I won't be doing much work for a while. It's all on you now buddy."

"I can handle it. I just want you to get better. You need to rest now."

I comforted Cassie as well as I could, then ran over to Aaron's house to get his wagon. Jesse came back with me and we put Cassie and Ella into the wagon and we made our way to Dr. Reed's home which was about three miles away.

"The bullet passed clean through. She was lucky though. It could've been much more serious. The bullet could have struck an artery or somewhere else more serious. She was very lucky Micah," said Dr. Reed.

The following days are still foggy to me. I realized that the bullet was meant for me and that the trouble was not going to go away. I knew I had to make a decision.

If I'd lost Cassie, my life would no longer have had much meaning. Of course, I would've had Ella but I came close to losing the love of my life. I was scared. I knew I had to do something.

After several days, when Cassie was feeling better, I informed her that I had made a decision. "Cassie, we're leaving the farm. I can't keep you and Ella here any longer. I don't think it's safe for us to stay here. I'm going to talk with Mother and Aaron and then we're going to leave. I don't know for how long but I'll let them use our farm while we're gone."

"Whatever you think best, Micah. I don't feel safe here now," Cassie said.

I went to see Mother and Aaron the next day. They were working behind the house when I approached. "Mother, Aaron, we're going to be leaving for a while. We need to get away. I think maybe we'll go to Charleston. Aaron, you and Jesse can work the farm if you want to. We're all family. Whatever you produce is yours. But, we have to go. I don't think it's safe for me or the girls here any longer. Those men may still be looking for revenge. We need to leave right away."

"Okay Micah," Aaron said. We'll take good care of the farm until you return. We're going to miss you but we do understand. Take good care of Ella and Cassie."

"We love you Micah. Please be safe," Mother said. Come back and see us when you can. Maybe we'll come see you in Charleston."

Chapter 73

We did leave a few days later but we never returned. Past memories, especially the attack on Cassie were much too painful for me to remember or to go back. Being away from the farm would be good for Ella and Cassie too, I thought. It would be a new beginning for all of us.

As it turned out, Charleston was a good decision for us. I was always handy with tools so I ended up doing carpentry in and around town. There was always plenty to do working on houses, doing new construction and repairing boats down at the docks. Charleston was growing and it was a good time to be there. The work kept me busy and allowed me to take care of the family.

Cassie did some sewing and other work for the local townspeople but mainly concentrated on raising our daughter. Our family had a wonderful relationship being together and at home every night. I now had the quiet, pleasant life that I had always dreamed of on my farm had circumstances not intervened.

Ella grew up to be a pretty, well-mannered, educated young lady. She was bright and had a wonderful demeanor like her mother. She met a young Army Captain in Charleston, got married and after about a year moved away. We knew that day would come but it was still painful for us when it occurred. I see her every few years but she's busy raising her own family now. She gave me four wonderful grandsons: Cole, Noah, Zachary and Jacob.

They never found the person who fired the shot that night. I really didn't think that they would but I wasn't eager to ask a lot of questions or reveal my new location to others. I just wanted to get away and be forgotten if that was possible. I assumed it was someone connected to the raiders we surprised that night in Savannah. I have no doubt however that the bullet fired that day was intended for me. As I look back at it now, I know that thankfully, it wasn't an assassin's bullet that took my Cassie's life that night but instead it was pneumonia, following a long illness in her later years. We lived many happy years together after that awful night.

AFTERWORD

I had just finished telling my story to Dr. Reynolds when he gave me a curious look. "There's a Miss Ali in the colored wing of the home and I would like for you to meet her. You're both from the same county and you seem to have been there at about the same time. I'm visiting with her tomorrow morning and I would like you to join me."

"Yes, I said I would like that."

The following morning, Dr. Reynolds and I entered the colored wing and walked down a long hallway. It was interesting to see this side of the home because I had heard about it from the nurses and attendants but had never been inside.

I noted soft singing, probably a religious gospel song coming from a room a few doors up on the left. As it turned out, that was where we were going.

"Doesn't Miss Ali sing nicely Micah?" Dr. Reynolds asked.

"She sure does."

After saying that, I looked closely at her and she seemed to look back at me with the same gentle stare. "Aliyah, is that you?" I asked with astonishment.

"Yes, I'm Aliyah. You look familiar sir but do I know you? Unfortunately, I don't see as well as I used to."

"It's me, Micah. Remember, we lived on the farm together."

"Gracious God can it be you?" she gasped.

"Yes, it is me, Daniel's brother. I'm older now and I'm sure I've changed since you last saw me."

"Come closer please. Why yes, you have changed a bit. But you're still every bit as handsome as the young man I once knew."

"I think I'll make my rounds and let you two visit for a while," Dr. Reynolds said, as he got up and walked from the room.

"How are you Aliyah? How has your life been? I haven't seen you since that day I said goodbye to you at the church.

"I know. We expected to see you again but you never came back. We wondered what had happened to you."

"Someone shot at us through the window of our home one night a few weeks later, probably as revenge for my helping the church back then so I decided to leave the farm for a while. I eventually sold it and never returned. Cassie and I raised our daughter Ella in Charleston. It was a good place for us."

"My husband, Elijah passed away about five years ago," Aliyah said. "I have a son, Isham who is doing well. He's in his 50's now and has a family of his own. He's my oldest and I also have two daughters, Rebecca and Sarah. My son works for the railroad and my daughters are both teachers. Isham is coming to visit this Saturday, he comes every weekend. I'd like for you to meet him."

"I'd like that very much." After about an hour of reminiscing, I left her room and headed back to my wing of the home. Before leaving, I asked Aliyah if I could visit her from time to time and she said that would be wonderful. She looked good and like me, somewhat slowed by years but I was so happy to see her again, after all this time. I knew I would have trouble sleeping that night. I figured I'd be up all night remembering those days.

Saturday morning arrived and I headed over toward the colored wing of the home. As I was heading in that direction, a white resident sitting in the hallway asked me, "Where're you going?"

"I'm going to see someone," I said with a smile.

"You don't belong over there. You should stay out," he said.

"I'm visiting a very dear friend and you should mind your own damn business," I said softly, with a stern facial expression. I then continued to walk toward Aliyah's wing.

I arrived close to ten that morning and as I had before, I knocked on the door gently and said, "Miss Ali".

"Come in," she replied.

As I entered slowly, I noticed a man sitting in the chair next to her. He was dressed nicely and I noticed that he had a much lighter complexion than Aliyah.

"Hello Sir, I'm Isham. Mother said you were coming today. It's nice to meet you," he said, extending his hand in greeting to me. I didn't remember Isham from my time in Savannah so he must have been born afterwards, I thought.

"Isham, it's very nice to meet you. I knew your Mother from Savannah many years ago. She tells me that you work for the railroad."

"Yes, I've worked there for about twenty-five years."

Aliyah interrupted. "Does he look familiar to you, Isham?"

"Yes, I think so but I'm not sure why. Did I know you when I was young?" he asked me.

Aliyah interrupted again, "No, does he look familiar to you Isham?" She paused, "He should he's your Uncle Micah. He's your father's brother."

It was quite a revelation for both of us and we had to let our thoughts settle for a moment.

"Wow, I don't know what to say," said Isham.

"Your father would have been very proud of you," I said.

"I would really like to hear about my father, if you'll tell me about him."

"I will," I said, as I got up and went over, giving him a big bear hug. I stepped back a little. "I can tell you two things right now. Your father was the best soldier I ever served with in the army and your mother was the sweetest woman I ever knew."

Isham smiled.

"What is that pleasant smell?" I asked.

"Isham, give your Uncle Micah that dish I asked you to bring today," Aliyah said.

"Wow, cornbread and molasses. You remembered after all these years," I said, looking at Aliyah.

"I remembered that it was your favorite growing up," she said.

"Thank you. I know I'll enjoy this." After visiting with them for a few hours, I said, looking at Isham, "We'll visit again soon and I'll tell you all about your father. I need to be getting back now. They'll come looking for me if I'm away too long," I said smiling. "Miss Ali, I'll be back again soon I promise. I then looked over at Isham, "Please come to see me whenever you want. We have a lot to talk about. It was really special meeting you."

As I walked toward the door with tears in my eyes, I turned to Aliyah and whispered, "Thank you."

I left the room that day feeling like the sun was shining for me for the first time in a while. My quiet, almost empty existence just a few days earlier was changing. I felt like I had something new to live for--a related family with ties to my past with whom I could share my remaining years. I couldn't wait to write Ella with my good news.

Glenn Ogden - Bio

The author has always had a strong interest in history, especially the American Civil War and the impact it had on the lives of the people who lived during that period. Glenn's background includes service in the U. S. Army and human resources in the communications industry. This is his first novel. Glenn and his wife Lynne reside in South Florida.

Made in the USA
Charleston, SC
11 December 2016